HOW TO MEASURE TRAINING EFFECTIVENESS

How to Measure Training Effectiveness

Leslie Rae

Gower

Published by
Gower Publishing Company Limited,
Gower House,
Croft Road,
Aldershot,
Hants GU11 3HR,
England
Reprinted 1987

British Library Cataloguing in Publication Data

Rae, Leslie
How to measure training effectiveness.
1. Employees, Training of—Evaluation
I. Title
658.3'12404   HF5549.5

ISBN 0–566–02596–5

Printed in Great Britain at the University Press, Cambridge

CONTENTS

Page

Preface   ix

1 **Where do we start?**   1
Definitions — Reasons — Trainer interest —
Training Manager interest — Senior management interest — Client interest — Questions
for validation and evaluation.

2 **In the beginning.**   11
Identification of training needs — Who
identifies needs — Analysis — Job analysis —
Job description — Job specification — Training
specification — Training objectives — Aims
and objectives.

3 **Detailed analysis.**   26
Knowledge analysis — Other analyses —
Observational analysis — Observation support
interviews — Unstructured interviews —
Structured interviews — Co-counselling —
Questionnaires — Delphi technique —

Audits — Diary method — Critical incident technique — Brainstorming — Mirroring — Psychological tests.

4 Techniques of analysis: the Repertory Grid. 42
Aims of the Repertory Grid — In practice — Interviewer help — Problems.

5 Techniques of analysis: Observational methods. 56
Process observation — Behaviour observation — Behaviour categories — Definitions of categories — Behaviour observation forms — Analysis of the interaction.

6 Now we're ready to train. 70
Control groups — Initial assessments — Knowledge/Skill assessment — Knowledge tests — Open answer — Binary choice — Multiple choice — Short answer — True/False choice — Skills assessment — Semantic Differential Questionnaire — Thurstone Scale — Likert Scale — Self-assessment of attitudes.

7 Assessments during the event. 86
Activity observation — Aids to observation — Audio equipment — Video equipment — Behaviour analysis — Course audits — Session assessments — Tutor assessments — Over-use of tests.

8 End of event validation. 103
Internal validation approaches — Group review — End-of-course questionnaires — Feelings review — Action planning — Interview approach — Immediate or delayed validation — External validation approaches — Validation of knowledge increase — Validation of skills — Practical application — Behaviour analysis —

Repertory Grid — Semantic Differential
Questionnaire — the 3-Test approach.

9 After the euphoria.   125
Delayed evaluation approaches — Inclusion
of other people — Control groups — Action
planning — Indirect observation questionnaires — Direct observation — Depth interviews — Repertory grid — Self-diaries — Business assessment — Value for money — Long-
term evaluation — Techniques — Who does
the evaluation?

Appendix One.   The evaluation process   139

Appendix Two.   Practical applications   141

References and recommended reading   144

Index   149

PREFACE

'I don't know how to start', 'I don't know what to do', 'Why should I do it?', 'It's going to take a lot of time/money', 'I haven't the time'. Such are the remarks commonly heard when questions of the validation and evaluation of training are raised. It has always surprised me that so much training, in whatever form, is embarked upon without any thoughts of validation or evaluation other than an optimistic 'It sounds just what we want'. Has it been firmly established *what* is needed? Is the proposed approach the most appropriate one? Is the course *known* to be the most suitable? How will we be able to find out what the result of the training will be? There are so many questions which need to be asked both before and after the event.

This book sets out to suggest ways – from the initial stages to long after the training itself has finished – in which any form of training can be assessed for effectiveness and value – validation and evaluation. In it I summarise the different approaches necessary at each stage of the process and wherever possible suggest practical instruments, usually based on my own experiences.

The book is intended as a practical guide, rather than an academic approach, to the subject and will be found useful by trainers, training managers, and non-trainers who require assessments to be made. All stages from the training concept to long-term evaluation are included, although the full range of stages need not be necessary on every occasion – some may have already been applied and the information obtained. The approaches described include those which can be applied to singular events or to complete training programmes. In other words, to any situation which demands answers to the questions 'Is it effective? Is it worthwhile?'

To anyone with doubts about setting off on the validation/ evaluation trail, the advice I would give is 'go ahead and do something'. Whatever may be done, however minimal, will produce some positive benefit. Many situations are themselves so subjectively based that any assessment itself must be similarly subjective. If a subjective assessment is all that is available, go ahead and obtain it, although try to reduce its subjectivity as far as possible. After all, it may be impossible to obtain an assessment which is more objective; so, in these cases, a controlled, subjective assessment may be better than none at all.

The list of recommended books and other publications is far from exhaustive, at least as far as published articles and papers is concerned, although not a lot has been published about the subject – probably because not a great deal of validation and evaluation is sought.

Finally, a word about gender. In writing the text I have not gone to the ridiculous lengths of making everybody plural to avoid the 'he/she' trap. The terms 'he/she', 'her/ his', 'him/her' and 'herself/himself' are usually abbreviated to the neutral, simple descriptions 'he', 'his', 'him' and himself'.

Any opinions expressed, unless otherwise indicated, are my own and do not necessarily represent the views of my present employer, the Manpower Services Commission.

Leslie Rae

1
WHERE DO WE START?

Many statements have been made concerning the feasibility of validation and evaluation. In many areas of training it has been said that validation and evaluation are very difficult, if not impossible to achieve. The areas usually referred to in this context are the general aspects of management training or human relations training. In other words, all forms of training in which it cannot be shown completely objectively or quantitatively that the trainee has learned to add two plus two (or its equivalent) to produce four on x number of occasions. Training of this nature usually has problems which have a right answer and the direct validation and evaluation relate to the performance of the learner in respect of the learning – if the lessons have been taught well and the trainee has learned the lessons to the satisfaction and measurement of the trainer, the effectiveness of the training has been validated. Evaluation is also straightforward, since, if the learner always, as a result of the training, produces the answer four to our original question, he is always right and thus does not cost his employer as a result of expensive mistakes.

Let us look at a different form of training. A manager is attending a course which is aimed at developing counselling techniques and skills. Note the word 'developing', since few managers will attend the course with no skills whatsoever, either learned or inherited. At the end of the course a manager can perform an interview in a manner acceptable to the trainer. But another manager might interview in some way at variance to the model presented and produce results which, in the trainer's eyes, are not satisfactory but *are* in the view of the interviewer. We shall leave the interviewee out of the equation as he is just a complication factor! Do these results validate or invalidate the training and who is to make the pronouncement? The wider aspects are even more difficult to assess. Back at work the trainees cited above will counsel members of their staff in private. We do not know whether they use the techniques presented on the course; we do not know how successful the interview really was; we do not know whether, as a result of the interview, how successful and more effective the interviewee might be, and so on. We can guess; we can ask both parties for their views; we can observe. But is this sufficient to qualify as absolute validation and evaluation in the strictest sense of the words? I believe not.

So let us start from the premises that validation and evaluation

- are possible in some forms of training
- are very difficult in other forms of training
- are impossible in fully objective and quantitative terms in some forms of training.

We should firstly ensure that we know what we mean when we use the words validation and evaluation, as well as the word assessment which is often substituted if people are uneasy with the other terms. The 'real' meanings of these words have probably been discussed in training circles more than any other training terms, and with little positive results.

DEFINITIONS

The Manpower Services Commission has published a 'Glossary of Training Terms' which provides two definitions used by many trainers as the basis for discussion, although they are little more than the views of the Glossary's anonymous compiler.

The MSC definitions for validation are:

'1. Internal validation. A series of tests and assessments designed to ascertain whether a training programme has achieved the behavioural objectives specified.

2. External validation. A series of tests and assessments designed to ascertain whether the behavioural objectives of an internally valid training programme were realistically based on an accurate initial identification of training needs in relation to the criteria of effectiveness adopted by the organisation.'

The definition given for evaluation is

'The assessment of the total value of a training system, training course or programme in social as well as financial terms. Evaluation differs from validation in that it attempts to measure the overall cost benefit of the course or programme and not just the achievement of its laid down objectives. The term is also used in the general judgemental sense of the continuous monitoring of a programme or of the training function as a whole.'

And finally the MSC definition for 'Assessment of Training Effectiveness' is given as

'A general term for the process of ascertaining whether training is efficient or effective in achieving prescribed objectives. It covers both evaluation and validation.'

Dictionary definitions are respectably vague. To validate is to 'make valid (sound, defensible, well-grounded), ratify, confirm', and to evaluate is to 'ascertain amount of, find numerical expression for, appraise, assess.'

Warr, Bird and Rackham were concerned with evaluation only and saw evaluation as being used in a wider context than in the MSC definitions. They saw two basic aspects of evaluation – input evaluation and outcome evaluation. Input evaluation considers the question 'What procedures are most likely to bring about change?' and covers the questions which need to be asked before a training event can be organised. Such questions will relate to training aspects over which the trainer has control and choice such as

- which training approach?
- external or internal resources?
- format of the event?
- type of learner to be invited?

Outcome evaluation is described in terms which many people will see as a combination of validation and evaluation and is concerned with identifying, from evidence, changes which have occurred as a result of the training. Various levels of evaluation are described – immediate reaction, immediate outcome, intermediate and ultimate outcomes. From the point of view of the Manpower Services Commission definitions, the immediate outcome and immediate reaction levels are approaches more inclined to the validation of training, and the intermediate and ultimate outcome levels more in terms of the wider aspects of evaluation.

Hamblin dismissed the MSC definitions as suggesting differences between validation and evaluation which were not always meaningful. He defines evaluation as 'any attempt to obtain information (feedback) on the effects of a training programme and to assess the value of the training in the light of that information.' As with Warr, Bird and Rackham's comments, Hamblin's use of 'evaluation' is a comprehensive term to include both of the MSC definitions.

REASONS

Whatever definition we place on the words which describe what we are doing, or should be doing, our intention must be to determine certain facts in order to gauge the success of our training. The argument will still remain as to whether we should be determining this success or measuring it, but what we want to know must attempt to answer certain questions.

(a) Has the training satisfied its objectives?
(b) Has the training satisfied the needs of the clients?

(c) Are people operating differently at the end of, and as a result of, the training?
(d) Did the training contribute directly to this different behaviour?
(e) Is the learning achieved being used in the real work situation?
(f) Has the learning contributed to the production of a more effective and efficient worker?
(g) Has the training contributed to a more effective and efficient (hence more cost-effective) organisation?

These questions fall naturally into two aspects related to the training: questions a, b and c are concerned with the training itself more than anything else, whereas d,e,f and g are more concerned with the effect of the training on the work.

This approach correlates well with the basic MSC definitions, namely in that validation is concerned with the efficiency of the training and evaluation with its effectiveness when applied to work. Such an approach may appear simplistic, but it attempts to separate two elements which can so easily become confused and hence cause confusion. This approach will form the basis of the methods recommended in this book.

If there are so many problems connected with validation and evaluation, why should we consider attempting to resolve them? The need stems from a number of sources.

TRAINER INTEREST

If we are performing a training function, and if we are at all concerned about our skill levels as trainers, and how we are able to help others to learn, we must want to know the extent of the efficiency and effectiveness of that training. This is not self-vindication but an essentially practical approach to confirm that

- our training ideas are in step with the learning needs
- our skills are being maintained
- the opportunity is available for us to improve.

It is only logical that we should consider these factors in order to obtain information. One of the major teaching points of the trainer, particularly if he is involved in human relations training, is that if an individual or an organisation is to be and to continue to be effective, there must be a regular supply of open feedback. Feedback in this instance is validation when it is measured against the desired objectives.

The trainer who is an independent consultant is at a disadvantage in obtaining feedback compared with the in-company trainer. The in-company trainer, in addition to the formal validation measures, also has recourse to the internal grapevine and direct or indirect contact with his trainees' bosses. He also knows that if things are going wrong there is a managerial element in the company hierarchy which will ensure that he is informed. The independent trainer has, to a major extent, to rely on the formal, written validation instruments alone. However, there is also another indicator available which should at least warn him that there are questions he should be asking of himself and others – that is his business indicator. Are former clients returning for more of the same training or the next stages in a progressive training plan, and/or is the supply of new clients drying up more quickly than might have been predicted? A negative response is not an answer in itself since a number of factors might be contributing to declining business, such as a declining economy, none of which is directly attributable to the trainer.

TRAINING MANAGER INTEREST

In the same way that the trainer has an interest in his own skills and acceptability, so has the training manager an interest in the level of performance of his trainers. He can and should be observing them directly in action. But these observations may not always be possible and when they are, they are made from a singular position. The manager's views may not reflect those of the people who matter – those under training. The views of the training clients are given in the validation instruments and the training manager will need to balance his views with those expressed in this way. His role in many ways is more difficult than that of the trainer: the training manager is responsible for ensuring that the training given satisfies the needs, but he is also himself a manager of people. The connecting lines attached to the manager extend up as well as down. He will have some form of senior management above him who will be interested in both validation and evaluation, but particularly evaluation. The interest from a validation point of view will be whether the training department is operating as an effective and efficient organisation. The training manager will certainly be called upon to produce evidence towards this, evidence which will need to be as objective and as quantitative as possible.

SENIOR MANAGEMENT INTEREST

In addition to having the internal interest through the training manager on the efficiency of the training department, an organisation's senior management will also have an interest in evaluation in the widest sense of this term. Once it has been satisfied that the training itself is effective, the senior level of management will want to know whether
- the training is being applied in the work situation
- the training is producing sufficient change in organisational efficiency to warrant the continuation of the training expenditure.

It is in this investigatory area of evaluation that least work is done because it is very difficult and time- and resource-consuming, particularly in the case of the training of managers and in human relations training. There are also strong links between evaluation of this nature and management development in the controlling hands of line management. It is rare for these investigations to be carried out fully and effectively, although lip service is frequently paid to the principle.

CLIENT INTEREST

Trainees taking part in a training programme have a number of needs in both the organisational and the personal development areas. The trainer needs to know if he is satisfying these needs and only the client can give advice on this.

In many cases the client accepts the training on trust. In the case of the organisation with a training department, the client accepts to a large extent that the training has been validated and evaluated by the organisation. But a rather more informal system of validation and evaluation exists and cannot be ignored, although it may not necessarily be accurate. This is the internal grapevine which can produce such evaluatory statements as 'I wouldn't go on that course if I were you, it's a waste of time' or 'It was a super course, but of course I haven't done anything with what we talked about' or 'That training changed my whole outlook and I can do everything so much better now.'

The grapevine can work equally for or against the external training consultant and often it is only the word of mouth validation and evaluation which may clinch a contract. If the Managing Director who is considering a training event has a Managing Director friend with previous experience of the training consultant being considered, the friend's comments will result in either acceptance or rejection. Perhaps a less biased method of obtaining information about training organisations or individual consultants is to obtain assessments, if these are available, from an organisation such as the Management Training Index which collates the (albeit subjective) views of people who attend courses run by organisations which support the Index.

QUESTIONS FOR VALIDATION AND EVALUATION

Questions also arise in validation and evaluation, but particularly the former, as to what aspects of a training course should be assessed. Possible aspects will include

Content of training. Is it relevant and in step with the training needs? Is it up to date?

Method of training. Were the methods used the most appropriate ones for the subject? Were the methods used the most appropriate for the learning styles of the participants?

Amount of learning. What was the material of the course? Was it new to the learner or merely the mixture as before? Was it useful, although not new to the learner, as confirmatory or revision material?

Trainer skills. Did the trainer have the necessary attitude and skill to present the material in a way which encouraged learning?

Length and pace of the training. Given the material essential to learning, was the learning event of the appropriate length and pace? Were some aspects laboured and others skimped?

Objectives. Did the training satisfy its declared objectives? Was the learner given the opportunity to try to satisfy any personal objectives? Was this need welcomed? Were personal objectives actually satisfied?

Omissions. Were any essential aspects omitted from the learning event? Was any material included which was not essential to the learning?

Learning transfer. How much of the learning is likely to be put into action on return to work? If it is to be a limited amount only or none, why is this? What factors will deter or assist the transfer of the learning?

Accommodation. If course accommodation is within the control of the trainer, or is relevant to the type of training event, he may wish to ask whether the hotel/conference centre/training centre was suitable. Was the accommodation acceptable? Were the meals satisfactory?

Relevance. The final question in a validation assessment may be concerned with the relevance of the total training approach. Was this course/seminar/conference/workshop/tutorial/coaching assignment/project/etc. the most appropriate means of presenting a learning opportunity?

Questions of evaluation would, in the defined approach suggested, be concerned with subsequent matters of application of the learning. The questions asked might depend on the period of time which had elapsed between the training event and the evaluation.

Application of learning. Which aspects of your work now include elements which are a direct result of the learning event? Which new aspects of work have you introduced as a result of your learning? Which aspects of your previous work have you replaced or modified as a result of the learning? Which aspects of your learning have you not applied? Why not?

Efficiency. How much more efficient and/or effective are you in your work as a result of the training? Why/Why not? This question could also be posed to the learner's boss and his subordinates, but, as in so many cases, it will be highly subjective evidence and the questioning will need to be extensive.

Hindsight. With the passage of time and attempts to apply the learning, are there any amendments you would wish to make to your immediate outcome validation answers?

At the beginning of this chapter I suggested that we start with certain premises of possibility, difficulty and objective impossibility in attempting to evaluate and validate. The attitudes expressed so far do not change these views, but suggest that firstly we can attempt *some* form of validation and evaluation, however crude and sometimes necessarily subjective, and secondly we must attempt it, otherwise there is no measure at all in any form, of effectiveness in order to satisfy ourselves, our clients or others.

2
IN THE BEGINNING

One of the most commonly heard statements uttered by a senior manager about a new training programme, or in fact any new event in the organisation, is 'We must evaluate this . . . . .'. This view is very laudable and is one which I fully support. Unfortunately on so many occasions the statement is made during the event or even after its conclusion. Sometimes, however, it is made before the event starts, either the day before the event is due to commence or as a statement of intent about what should be done after the event. It is too late to consider evaluation at such times. Evaluation starts at the birth of the programme.

Let us consider the inception of a training programme. It is assumed (or hoped) that the training proposed is the result of an identified training need and not the consequence of the whim of a training officer or manager who likes the idea of presenting this form of training or the pronouncement of someone in high authority who feels that the company should be engaged in this type of training. Effective training starts with the identification of a need and it is also at this stage that evaluation starts. A training need stems from an equation which shows that a factor is missing and the training event supplies that missing factor. The existence of

11

a training need states that a change is necessary: a change from a situation or performance which is below that level required to at least the required level. The change agent is the training event.

IDENTIFICATION OF TRAINING NEEDS

What we have been considering is an existing level of achievement and an outcome level as the end result. In order to talk objectively about this approach we must have an assessment or measurement of these levels. If the level is -3 at the start of the process and the level is $+3$ at the end of the training, depending on the objectives, this positive change of 6 units demonstrates that the training has been effective.

The two aspects, therefore, go hand in hand – the identification of a training need means that performance is not up to the level required and this in turn means that both the existing level of achievement and that required have been measured and assessed.

Training needs can obviously be many and various depending on the nature of the job to be done and the people who have to peform the jobs. They can be expressed generally in terms of skills, attitudes and knowledge. Some needs may cover this whole spectrum while others, perhaps, may concentrate on singular aspects only. School-leavers entering an electronics manufacturing industry will probably have learning needs in all three areas – knowledge, skills and attitudes. They will need to be aware of such aspects of knowledge as the product range, the limits of the job they will be performing, the safety aspects applied to the job and so on. The processes they will need to perform will be new to them and they will need to learn the skills of operation and manipulation. At school their attitudes were possibly those of individual, scholastic achievement, whereas their new job will demand a close co-operation within a team – this may require a completely new approach to people, a change of social attitude.

On the other hand, machine operators changing companies may only need the new knowledge about the product they will be making and their new work environment, or they may only need the new skills necessary to operate a slightly different machine to which they have been accustomed. A history teacher, moving to a new school which uses more progressive teaching methods, may be fully skilled in these methods but may not have used them for a long time, certainly not in the previous school, so there may be required an adjustment of attitude to bring into use the different methods.

Some training needs are more straightforward to assess or measure than others. A manufacturing company is failing to meet its objectives by x per cent because of the lack of skill of its operatives: a meter reader is making 50 per cent errors or more because he does not know how to read the new meters: x per cent of students are reporting no progress from a training course because they are unable to understand the teacher's explanations. In the knowledge area, too many packages are going astray because there has been considerable staff movement and the porter does not know where everybody is now located. Attitude training needs are more difficult to define (and to satisfy) and in many cases must only be subjective assessments – 'Her team doesn't seem to be functioning well; probably because of a clash of personalities between y and z members'.

Too often these initial assessments are not looked at closely, either because nobody thinks there is a need to do so or the pressure (of various sorts) is such that assessment is not possible. In these cases, to look for eventual evaluation is to look for unreliable, completely subjective, or valueless results.

WHO IDENTIFIES NEEDS?

Training and development are areas in which there have been considerable movements over the past few years. I would prefer to say 'advances', rather than 'movements', but so little evaluation of the new approaches has taken place or has been possible, that to do so would be dangerous. These developments have been evident in the topics of training, the use of technology as training aids, and most of all in the increasing variety of approaches used. But perhaps the major development, and here I do believe 'advance' is appropriate although I cannot prove it, is in the ownership of the training.

A few years ago, training was almost exclusively trainer-centred. The trainer determined the objectives of the course, how long it would last, its content and its format. On many occasions the training was of a pedagogic nature with the trainer in complete control of the direction of the training. The views of the trainees were rarely sought, or if they were, they were sought in a very controlled manner and almost as if the trainer was saying 'Well, I suppose I should let *them* say something'. In recent years we have seen a progressive change in this approach through an increased receptiveness to the requested views of the trainees, then receptiveness to unsolicited views, resulting in events which are completely trainee-centred and directed, such as extreme forms of T-groups or encounter groups.

Course formats have also undergone similar liberations. From a completely trainer-conceived programme construction, approaches have swung towards the trainees who may be asked in specially conceived workshops to produce a course based on their requirements, or they may attend a course which they construct from their needs as they go along, within the confines only of the original *raison d'être*.

Similar movements can be applied to the identification of training needs. Traditionally, the role of the boss included the monitoring of the skills and so on of the people for whom he was responsible, and the identification of weaknesses and shortcomings. These would be 'remedied' by unilateral nominations of the offenders for remedial training courses, irrespective of any (unsought) views of the individual. With the introduction of a more neo-paternal approach to management, the training was discussed with the individual before nomination went ahead. There is no doubt that both these approaches still exist and they surface in the comments of students at the beginning of a course when they say 'I was sent', with the implication or even direct comment on occasions 'and I didn't want to come'. The inroads of real participative management are encouraging an increasingly common approach in which the training need is identified by the individual who then comes forward to discuss both the problem and possible solutions with the boss.

A see-saw effect takes place in some organisations where management development is a living organism. The self-application by individuals is in fact reduced by the line manager fulfilling his responsibilities and being actively interested and involved in the development of his staff. As a result the individuals are no longer left in a vacuum and forced to make their own applications. However, where Managing Director and OD work effectively in this way, the final 'nomination' for training is the result of a full discussion between the two parties, irrespective of who initiates the movement.

The Training Department may well now ask where it fits into the scheme for the identification of training needs – 'After all we are the training experts'. Much of course will depend on the identified and agreed role of the department in the organisation concerned and the distribution throughout the organisation of the necessary skills. There is much to recommend trainers conducting training needs surveys as they (or linked psychologists) may be the ones in the organisation with the skills necessary for conducting such surveys. The trainer is the one who is more likely to have the skills to conduct repertory grid interviews, for example, than line managers. The psychologist has a much more extensive and intensive knowledge of the construction of diagnostic questionnaires and so on. A major role for the trainer in these circumstances may be the use of his skills and expertise in helping the learners and their bosses to practise the processes. In this role the trainer can ensure maximum success but care must be taken not to usurp the rightful roles of the individual and the boss. After all, there will be considerably more commitment from the individuals if they make an important contribution to the end result. The role of the trainer will also increase in stature if guidance and help is given tactfully and professionally.

It can be argued readily that the line manager and the individual are in the best positions to identify the training needs. After all they are on the spot, know the work and should be able to identify quickly and easily any problems which may need a training solution. However, if the trainer accepts this argument completely his role will be reduced simply to a reactive agent, mounting any training demanded by the learner and his boss. A much more meaningful relationship will evolve if a partnership is produced between the three parties – learner, boss and trainer – each contributing their own special expertise. The stature of the trainer will grow as he develops the role of consultant as well as the provider of any training required. If a realistic view is taken, it must also be accepted that not every manager will be sufficiently motivated or even capable of identifying training needs. In such cases, the trainer will have a major role to play.

Whoever may identify the training needs, the process of identification is similar and can be expressed in the model shown in Figure 2.1, given below.

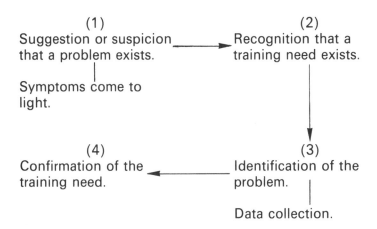

Figure 2.1   Identification of training needs

Stage 1 can be initiated in a variety of ways and often depends on where an organisation's responsibilities lie. Unless there is a routine mechanism which surveys training needs, many training needs come to light accidentally or as the result of some unrelated activity. A common situation which can suggest the existence of training needs is when shortfalls in service or production become evident in an organisation. These can suggest that the job is not being performed correctly at some stage, perhaps due to a shortfall in skills, knowledge or attitudes in the job performers. Of course the shortfall may have nothing to do with training needs at all, but once the warning signals have been given, some form of investigation is a logical step which may be taken quite naturally. Audits, whether financial or general, can also be occasions when shortfalls are discovered and usually an immediate identification of whether or not they are due to a training problem can be made.

It should not be assumed, of course, that a shortfall in skill, knowledge or attitude means that there is necessarily a training problem. This will be confirmed at Stage 2. Failure to perform effectively can be identified with one of two causes. The failure or deficiency may be due to a lack of training or ineffective training, or it may simply be due to a lack of execution – the individual has the skill or knowledge to perform the task but either fails or refuses to perform. One of the principal problems connected with training which has taken place off the job is the transfer of that learning to the job. If the individual has been trained effectively but still fails to perform effectively, further training will be useless and the problem requires a more direct line management approach.

However, training needs will arise from the identification of a deficiency in a routine inspection or survey, or result from a special survey mounted to determine whether any training needs might exist.

Stage 4 introduces the in-depth analysis of the training need related to recommendations for its fulfilment, and is characterised by two major aspects of the process of training needs identification – job analysis and data collection.

ANALYSIS

If we are to identify what is wrong with a job or a person performing a job, before we can rectify the situation we must be fully aware of the extent and nature of the job or role. This is obtained or confirmed by an analysis of what is actually occurring. In this process there are more titles with conflicting and vague definitions than we found when considering evaluation and validation.

The three major aspects of analysis which can be considered the most useful in identifying training needs are job analysis, task analysis and skills analysis. These various aspects of analysis are arranged in descending order of describing the magnitude of extent – job relates to the full range of tasks which are required to be performed which in turn require specific skills. In an analysis of training needs there are advantages in following this order.

JOB ANALYSIS

At the initial stage of the analysis we require an overall, but detailed description of the activities and requirements of the whole job, for example, that of a hotel receptionist, a wages clerk, a capstan lathe operator and so on. Obviously there should be a number of existing aids which can save a considerable amount of background knowledge build-up. The most useful of these should be what is known as the job description. I say 'should' since, in spite of the value of this document and exhortations that one should always be provided, it tends to be a rarity which has either never existed or is described as 'kept here somewhere since we wrote it fifteen years ago'.

Otherwise, the training needs analyst will have to build up his own view of the job description or rely on published descriptions of jobs.

JOB DESCRIPTION

Job descriptions are statements of the outline of the whole job and show the duties and responsibilities involved in that job. The pattern of job descriptions varies when we go beyond this basic statement and they can include entries about lines of communication, hours of work, pay and other conditions to such an extent that they may overlap the contract of employment. For the purpose of a training needs analysis we shall be concerned principally with those parts of the description which relate to the operation of the job. However, entries which relate to lines of communication or, more significantly, the absence of these may be a first indication where a shortfall exists.

An example of a job description for a hotel receptionist is given in Figure 2.2.

Job title:	Hotel receptionist.
Function:	To maintain the hotel's bookings, reservations and charge system and be the hotel's principal customer contact point.
Lines of Communication:	Upwards – to head receptionist. Laterally – to other receptionists. Downwards – to junior receptionist and hall staff.
Responsibilities:	To – head receptionist. For – junior receptionist.
Hours of work:	Shift system (detailed according to practice).
Duties:	1. Dealing with room reservations made by telephone, letter, Telex and customer contact.
	2. Allocating reservations and completing records of these reservations.
	3. Confirming reservations with customers by the relevant means.

Figure 2.2 Example of a job description

When the job description is being used for the purposes of training needs analysis, the duties section will be the most important part of the description as this describes what the individual worker is required to do and should be able to do. The description of duties in a job description should be complete, including an additional section showing 'occasional duties' and should be expressed in terms as simple and unambiguous as possible without going into long descriptions of each task.

Probably the first step to be taken by the training needs analyst is to read the job description and observe the person performing the duties so that these duties and their relationship to each other are fully understood.

JOB SPECIFICATION

By this stage the analyst should have a good overall knowledge of the job in which he is interested: the duties have been listed in a job description and these are understood. It may be at this stage that training needs have become apparent. The job description is what the job holder *should* do and *should* be capable of doing. It may be obvious that an individual does not perform a particular duty because they do not know how to do it. The training function may then be simply to train the individual from a position of not being able to perform a task to being able to do so. This could be an example for a relatively simple case of validation and evaluation.

The simple need stated is most likely to occur in an analysis of the needs of new or relatively new workers: it is necessary to delve more deeply when the needs of more experienced individuals are involved. This is where the job specification and the action leading up to it can be most valuable.

A job specification details the skills, knowledge and attitudes which are required by the individual in order to carry out the duties involved in the job. For example, one duty of a painter and decorator may be paperhanging in which case the job specification would look, in part, like Figure 2.3.

Job title: Painter and decorator.
Duties: 3.   Paperhanging
                3.1 Task: Selection of paper.
                     Knowledge: types of wallcovering
                        including strengths, textures etc.
                     Skills: ability to assess covering by
                        manual manipulation.
                3.2 Task: measuring room.
                     Knowledge: methods of estimation;
                        unit methods of measurement.
                     Skills: measuring in various unit
                        methods.

Figure 2.3   Example of a job specification

In the job specification shown as an example in Figure 2.3 attitudes have not been listed. These will vary in their importance from job to job. In the case of the painter and decorator who may have to hang paper in private households the attitudes necessary will include patience, good social skills and awareness, a good attitude to hygiene both personal and in respect of the environment in which the work is being performed, and so on.

The more detailed the job specification, the easier it will be to identify where any deficiencies may lie. Obviously for some occupations the job specification will be long and detailed, whereas for others it will be relatively simple. However, the training needs analyst will certainly find that even fewer job specifications exist than job descriptions and it will often be necessary to construct them from scratch. There is no easy way to do this end and the operation will include

-   observation of the work
-   discussion in some form with the worker.

Some of the methods used in job data collection will be discussed in the next chapter as it is in this area that the analyst has the luxury of being able to select his own approaches.

TRAINING SPECIFICATION

At the end of the job specification stage, which will include data collection in order to permit task, skill and knowledge analysis leading to a full and detailed analysis of the job, any deficiencies will be apparent. Not only will the deficiency be apparent but also the extent of the shortfall, whether total, 50 per cent or minimal. This assessment leads to the general training specification which details the existence and extent of the training need. However, before these needs can be translated into training, it is necessary to determine the training objectives – clear statements of what the training should achieve.

TRAINING OBJECTIVES

The training objectives for any form of training must result directly from the job analysis and training specification and, to have any meaning, must be stated tightly, as quantitatively as possible, and behaviourally expressed so that any changes can be observed. Objectives of this nature not only give the lead to the actual training necessary, but also to the main theme of this book, namely validation and evaluation.

Let us return again to the case of the hotel receptionist. It has been found from feedback that she has errors in 90 per cent of any arithmetical calculations she has to do. The job description showed that a part of her duties was the calculation of customers' incidental accounts and the job specification showed that she needed to be able to do simple arithmetical calculations. Subsequent stages of the analysis showed that she was in fact poor at arithmetic, but a calculator was available for her use. Unfortunately nobody had ever explained the functions of the calculator to her; consequently she never used it and 'got her sums wrong'. The more this error occurred the greater became her panic and she was on the point of resigning. There was an obvious training need in this case, which, if the basic educational weakness of arithmetic was not to be tackled, when translated into training objective terms would be to teach the reception-ist to operate a calculator in the addition mode only so that she will be able to summarise customers' incidental expense accounts to 100 per cent accuracy, even under stress conditions.'

This objective is obviously the start of the validation and evaluation process. At the present time she is making 90 per cent errors. The training specification will contain a recommendation for training in the use of a calculator and the objectives will spell this out in specific terminal terms. A recommendation might also be made that she is helped in her general arithmetical ability by either a training course in this subject or perhaps assistance for her to attend day release or evening classes through further education.

The training can be validated easily on its completion by examination of terminal tests which will show whether she is able to use a calculator to the required efficiency level and thus whether the objectives have been achieved. When she returns to her work and continues to perform to the required level, evaluation has also been satisfied because she will be saving her employer money. Achievement and maintenance of the objective will also allow her to remain in a job which she enjoyed and for which she was otherwise very suitable.

AIMS AND OBJECTIVES

In training spheres, even among trainers who ought to know better, aims and objectives are often confused. It is not pedantry to comment in this way when the confusion is taken into the training and its evaluation. We considered earlier whether evaluation is only possible if the training need shortfall has been identified precisely at the start of the exercise. The aim is a statement of general intent whereas the objective states the requirement in precise terms. As an example of the differences between aims and objectives:

Aims are general statements of intent which give the global approach to the problem but without exact definition – 'I shall learn to fly'. This statement is an example of a general aim which is well short of exact definition. The aim concerned with flying does not state 'what' I shall learn to fly, in what period of time, to what level of competence, and it is even so vague and imprecise that it may mean that I have grown wings and intend to learn how to use them!

Objectives on the other hand are specific and precise statements of intent with precise measures of terminal behaviour. 'I shall learn to fly a jet fighter aeroplane by the end of next month to acrobatic display standards' is a much more precise statement of my intentions which on completion can be monitored and evaluated.

Within objective setting there are general principles to be followed. For an objective to have some degree of realism it will include

- a precise statement of the complete terminal behaviour required
- a statement of a conditions under which the performance is to be achieved
- a description of the standards to be attained.

Much has been written about the actual writing of objectives and the words and format to be used. One of the most useful publications on this subject is 'Preparing Objectives for Programmed Instruction' by Robert F. Mager (Fearon 1962), later re-titled 'Preparing Instructional Objectives' (Fearon 1975). Mager identifies words which, because they are open to ambiguous interpretation, should not be used in objective writing, such as 'to know', 'to appreciate', 'to understand', and so on.

Advice such as that given by Mager is important and, if followed, ensures that objectives are written which are not open to misunderstanding and specify the exact nature of what is to be achieved. However, what can (and does) happen is that people become so immersed in the pedantic complexities of ensuring that the words and the construction of an objective are 'correct' that the meaning of the objective is lost. Obviously the more specific and unambiguous the terms of the objective might be, the easier it will be to validate that objective and hence the training. But we should not become slaves to the construction of objectives: it is the 'result' of the training that matters, not its description.

If the three principles cited earlier are followed, the objective will satisfy its requirement whatever the words used. Purists will shudder at this acceptance of a greater generalisation, but it will certainly appeal to practising trainers who find it difficult to work to academic criteria as well as achieving the training, even though they may applaud the intent.

3
DETAILED ANALYSIS

Some of the methods of obtaining the details for a job specification were mentioned briefly in the preceding chapter; 'briefly' not because these methods are unimportant – quite the reverse as they will involve the greater part of an investigator's time. Rather they are very wide-ranging and varied, some are simple and some are highly sophisticated techniques requiring expertise and experience.

Much will depend on the nature of the problem presented as to which type of analysis will be the most appropriate and to whom. It may be that the training needs are group or organisation wide, or they may be confined to an individual, or an individual may be identified to take part in the analysis as a representative of the larger group.

KNOWLEDGE ANALYSIS

To determine knowledge levels and needs will require a different approach to an analysis of skills and is probably the most straightforward of the analytical approaches. Whether the approach is to an individual or a group, the analytical method consists of simple questioning to elucidate whether the required knowledge exists, observation that a set of rules or information is being followed or, in more complicated cases, a test can be set.

Although the approach will be relatively straightforward, it is necessary for the analyst to set clearly his objectives for the exercise. The criteria he will need to satisfy will include

- what is the range of knowledge to be tested?
- what questions are to be asked? What form will they have to take?
- what answers are required?
- how detailed are the answers required to be?
- what percentage of accuracy is required?
- who will assess the answers?
- how long can/should the questioning take?
- what should the environment be?

and so on.

The use of a knowledge analysis may, of course, come at a later stage than the initial establishment of training needs. It may be, for example, that an organisational needs analysis has identified a general need for training in Organisation and Methods techniques. Courses have been arranged, programmes produced (but on a flexible basis) and applications invited. Some time before the start of the first course the participants will have been allocated, but nothing is known about their level of knowledge of O and M techniques, except that someone has determined that they need the training. A questionnaire in the form of a test of knowledge can be sent out prior to the course to determine the level of knowledge of each participant. From the returned tests, the level of the course can be adjusted and base levels for eventual evaluation can be set.

An alternative to this approach is to retain the questionnaire until the students arrive on the course and to administer the test at an early stage, perhaps as the first activity of the course. This method ensures that all participants complete the test under identical conditions, but it also means that the tutors *must* be ready to modify the level of their inputs and activities immediately in the light of the information obtained.

One of the major problems of most training courses, except when completely new skills, concepts and so on are being introduced, is that those attending most courses will be heterogeneous as far as the knowledge level is concerned – there will be a range of knowledge between zero or almost zero to some degree of knowledge. It is the tutor's problem to set the level of the training at an intermediate level which will satisfy all. Unfortunately, if the range of knowledge is too wide there will be some who will feel that it is far too simple for them and others who will find the material too far above their heads for them to understand. For both these groups the course will not be an effective learning event. If however the waiting list for a particular type of training is large, the test can be given to all on the list. Course membership can then be adjusted as far as possible in the light of the test results. The only problem then is to ensure that the similar level people can be released for training at the same time – something which is frequently impossible for practical reasons!

OTHER ANALYSES

The analyses of skills and tasks, and particularly social skills and attitudes, are much more difficult to conduct and there must be considerable reliance on the observation and perception of others. Obviously the degree of difficulty and objectivity will depend on the skill and task being analysed. There is little doubt that management skills and attitudes, interpersonal or social skills, and attitudes generally will be the most difficult to assess.

OBSERVATIONAL ANALYSIS

Observation of the job or task being performed, and the person performing it, is the most readily available and the most commonly used method of analysis in most cases. Even so areas will still remain which do not lend themselves readily to practical observation. Such areas will include many of the personal staff interviews including appraisal interviews and similar events. It is unfortunate that it is these areas of management operation which often have most need of training.

Preparation must be thorough so that the observer knows exactly what is required from the observation since there may be problems in being able to return to cover something omitted on the initial occasion. It is normal to use an aide-memoire for most situations of this nature, but flexibility is very important and the observer must not feel that he is chained to the aide-memoire.

The first stage will involve the reading of the job description and a clarification of any doubtful areas. If the job is one with which the observer is not familiar, a talk with someone who is acquainted with the job can be useful, but this discussion must be kept at the strictly factual level in order to avoid contamination of the observer's views. The observer will need to be well acquainted with the job specification as the observations may disclose significant deviations from what should be happening. The job specification will also help in any decision about whether the whole job or only some tasks should be observed.

The next, essential stage is discussion with the person or group to be observed. The observed must be fully aware of when they will be observed, what the observer will be looking at and why the observation is taking place. Naturally, disclosure of this information to the person to be observed can have the effect of producing unnatural behaviour. An operator knowing he is being observed will take notice, for example, of all the safety checks he should perform (if he is aware of them). Two consequences may result from this effect.

(a) Perfect performance under observation has many similarities to training and it may be seen by the operator that the work proceeds as well or better if he does what he should be doing. This improved performance may be maintained without further training or emphasis.

(b) Unnaturally perfect performance as a result of observation may continue for an initial period only. Once the individual becomes involved in the task, natural reactions are more likely to occur as the observer will be ignored.

This is a common occurrence when television observation is used in training.

If the observation is not 'open', it may well result in either hostility, or suspicion and completely unnatural behaviour. It goes almost without saying that the relevant trade union(s) will have been brought in at an early stage and agreement reached. Without such co-operation the analysis could prove at best to be either abortive or an academic exercise, or, at worst, could produce adverse industrial relations.

Above all the analyst must have an objective approach. Great care must be taken in ensuring that what is noted is what the observer actually saw or heard – not what he wanted to see or hear. If it is possible, it is valuable to have the observations recorded in some way so that doubtful actions can be confirmed with objectivity. Recording is particularly useful when actions take place quickly and may possibly be missed in the observation.

As an example of observational analysis we may take one task of a hotel receptionist – the direct reception of new guests. Once the preliminaries cited above have been taken care of successfully, the analyst can take up a position where he can observe clearly, but not be too obtrusive to either the receptionist or the guest. In a situation of this kind there is only a little likelihood of observation contamination as the receptionist will be completely involved with the guest.

The work of the analyst begins when a guest enters the door and immediately pre-determined questions can start to be answered. Does the receptionist see the guest at this early stage and make any signs to this effect? If so, what? The customer walks across the floor between the entry and the reception desk. Is the receptionist doing any other work? What happens? Is obvious notice being taken of the approaching guest? And so on as the interaction continues. The initial actions described all relate to non-verbal skills and attitudes and can follow a pattern which is dictated by a general interpersonal philosophy, or a specific policy laid down by the employer.

Verbal behaviour is added to the non-verbal behaviour once the guest reaches the desk. What does the receptionist do or say? How is it said? What is the response? And so the interaction progresses with functional aspects being added to the behaviours to construct a total picture of how a customer is received.

Once the analysis is complete, it can be compared with the model of what should happen in an ideal situation. Any differences may indicate, if sufficiently substantial or important, a training need *or* a modification of the job specification or interactive model.

OBSERVATION SUPPORT INTERVIEWS

It is most unlikely that an observation alone will provide a complete analysis, particularly if there are significant differences observed from the job specification or model. In such a case, the analyst will want to know why the change occurred. The only way to obtain this information is to interview the person or persons being observed and ask why the deviation has taken place.

This personal contact with the observed subject must be done with tact and skill. If subjects are asked why they took a particular action, and it is obvious that their action differed from the 'official' action, answers might not be forthcoming and they might adopt a defensive stance. The questioning will have to be more circumspect and might usefully follow along the lines of: 'In such and such a circumstance, tell me what you do'. Supplementary questions of increasingly deeper levels could then cover the variation.

Interviews of this nature require a skilled interviewer/ analyst who has to be aware of the differences in the interactions involved, to be able to decide whether they are sufficiently significant to introduce, and to have interview skills sufficient to cope with any emerging problems. Considerable skill may be necessary to encourage the subject to talk freely, if only from the point of view of articulation. In the case of some subjects, for example the receptionist who is used to talking to strangers, this may not be difficult, but with other individuals whose work does not normally require them to talk about their work, bringing-out skills will be necessary. The interviewer must be a good listener and be adept at identifying 'clues' contained in the contributions made by the subject, and able to formulate questions which will develop these clues. Finally, the interviewer must be capable of assessing the information, sorting out the wheat from the chaff, and evaluating the significant information.

Unstructured Interview. This method of approach has just been described as the follow-up to an observation analysis, but it can stand alone as an investigatory event in job analysis and training needs analysis.

The subject of the job or task is obviously the focal point of the interview, but the interviewer has no set plan for the interview. He starts the worker talking about the job and by follow-up questions extracts the necessary information. An interview of this kind can take a long time but can be pleasing to both parties as it resembles a conversation more than a stereotyped interview.

As suggested earlier, the interviewer must be acutely alive to 'clues' being given by the interviewee and be able to develop these clues with probing questions or reflective approaches. A very common and much used question in this type of interview will be 'And what else can you tell me about that part of your job?'

A modification of the unstructured approach to the analysis interview can be the use of a semi-structured method. In this instance, the significant areas which the interviewer wishes to cover form the basis of the interview, but within this structure the interviewee is given considerable scope to respond freely. The interviewer is again listening carefully for clues to follow up and makes sure that by the end of the interview all his points have been considered, whatever useful side paths may have been followed. This method can be a most effective and enjoyable interview for both persons, as the interviewee is free to talk and the interviewer has at least a basic idea of the path the interview will take.

Structured Interview. The structured interview is probably the most common of the approaches in job and task analysis and if performed well can be a very effective vehicle for investigation. In this approach the interviewer plans the interview and particularly the nature and order of his questions in advance and in a logical sequence. 'What do you do first?'; 'Then what?'; 'What do you do after you have done x?'.

There are many advantages to this traditional approach to interviewing in that

- it usually takes less time than other approaches
- it is likely to avoid traumatic or awkward situations
- relatively unskilled interviewers find it an easier approach
- full information is usually obtained to the pre-determined questions.

There are, however, some disadvantages which are worth bearing in mind so that other approaches can be considered.

- it assumes that the interviewer knows all the questions to ask
- it is rigid and the interviewer will find difficulty in re-adjusting if the responses do not follow the assumed pattern
- clues may be ignored for the sake of maintaining the structure
- the interviewee may react against the formal approach even though the appropriate method of questioning is used.

Co-counselling. The approach described as co-counselling can be very useful when a number of people are involved in the analysis. Two of the subjects are brought together and invited to interview and counsel each other about their jobs and their training needs. If the results are to be useful from a job analysis point of view, there must be a written conclusion which can be used to summarise an analysis.

Although this method is less controlled than the other types of interview, much information can be obtained as there is no longer the potential analyst/subject barrier. The two people are talking together as colleagues and, provided the organisation's climate is right, will be free with each other and enjoy the interaction. The discussion may go deeper and wider than would be possible with an analyst.

The fact that this method is not analyst-centred has both advantages and disadvantages. The analyst has to be very careful when setting up the co-counselling pairs so that he explains the purpose of the exercise very clearly. Despite this, the individuals may not have the necessary interviewing or counselling skills to make the event work completely and to obtain all the information relevant to the exercise. There is also the possible problem of selecting incompatible pairs.

QUESTIONNAIRES

Interviews which are performed effectively usually yield a large amount of high quality information and data on which to base an analysis. However, in some cases this information may be suspect, as in the case when the information sought relates to the training needs of an organisation or a large group, rather than just the individual from whom the information was obtained. If the series of interviews was to be extended, it would be costly and time-consuming. If cost and time are at a premium, the interview approach may not be acceptable and the use of a questionnaire might be considered. The questionnaire approach will certainly be useful in determining levels of knowledge.

Where the analysis of skill is concerned, the use of a questionnaire is even more subjective than the interview and certainly more subjective than observation plus an interview. There are occasions in evaluation when we have to accept subjectivity and make the best use of it that we can.

A skills analysis questionnaire will be quite different from one used to assess knowledge. The only real variation possible in a knowledge questionnaire is in the method of response: a yes or no answer, a multiple choice, or an open response. In the case of skills there are also options possible in the form of the questions posed.

One approach will be to list the skills (and perhaps knowledge and attitudes) required for the job or task and ask the individual to state by a tick which skill is required in his opinion. The skills listed might be obtained from a job specification or even from an alternative questionnaire approach. The alternative approach is basically a plain sheet of paper on which the individual is asked to list the skills (knowledge or attitudes) required for the job. He could also be asked to rank them in order of importance or even to indicate his individual level of skill against each of the items.

Returning to the pre-determined data questionnaire, instead of a simple yes or no against the list of items, the completer could be asked to rate his own skill level against each item. This is particularly useful with a fully validated questionnaire where the individual's responses can be related to a norm.

Questionnaires used in skills analysis are quite different from those used in knowledge analysis. In the latter, the answers are usually either right or wrong. In an assessment of skills by questionnaire, other than skills which are almost synonymous with knowledge (for example some aspects of mathematics), the replies will be highly subjective since they are based on the views of the completer and could vary considerably, almost to extremes.

An attempt can be made to reduce the subjective element by extending the completion of the questionnaire to the subject's boss, his colleagues and, if possible or desirable, his subordinates. It must be established, however, that the other levels see enough of the subject's operation to make an objective assessment. Particularly in the case of the subordinates one must be certain that they have sufficient knowledge of the skills and functions on which to make an assessment. I have had subordinates whose assessment of my interpersonal skills on the basis of their criteria would not have pleased me and, on reflection, the same applies to some of the bosses I have had. Others could have similar views about me! The inherent dangers of this approach are therefore very real.

Questionnaires have other dangers. In particular they are not easy to construct in a readily understandable form, nor are they easy to produce in a universally valid and reliable format. They can, however, if necessary, reach a very wide sample of people and the large response is capable of relatively easy statistical analysis.

Delphi Technique. An extension of the questionnaire approach is afforded by the Delphi technique. In this approach the questionnaires, on return from a number of people, are tabulated and the distribution of the responses is demonstrated statistically. The distribution analysis is circulated among those who completed the questionnaire and they are asked, particularly those outside the middle range, whether they wish to reconsider their answers. The responses usually show a swing towards the middle range. The modified responses are again analysed according to the distribution and the completers of the questionnaires are again given another opportunity to revise their views. This approach is intended to ensure that all give the questionnaire their fullest consideration and that the opportunity is available for respondents to change their minds.

Audits. A further modification of the use of the questionnaire involves an approach known as an audit, for example, 'Management Development Audit'.

The purpose of an audit is to provide a clear picture of the state of affairs in a particular area of work prevailing in an organisation. If a picture of this nature is obtained, any deficiencies or training needs will show up as part of the audit. For example, if I wished to determine with regard to each management development system in an organisation

(a) to what extent it is practised
(b) an indication of its effective operation
(c) an indication of where training or further training is seen as necessary

an audit would supply most of this information.

The key to the difference between an audit and a straightforward questionnaire approach lies in the fact that the initial stages of an audit are linked with the objectives for the exercise.

Audits in this form have been pioneered by the Durham University Business School and they suggest that the area examined by an audit will produce analyses of

- involvement of the employee in the process
- communication of information
- planning
- assessment
- activity level.

The process starts when the organisation's senior management is interviewed in order to provide a clear picture of the organisation and its policy as determined by the management. This determination is essential so that the information subsequently obtained can be weighed against the stated policy. If no policy on particular aspects exists, it must be determined how assessments of effectiveness are made in practice and there must be a discussion of the audit so that top management is fully committed.

Once the base lines have been cleared, decisions are made about the practicalities of using the audit questionnaire. Pilot interviews are held with people in the organisation at the level at which the audit will be conducted so that the questionnaire can be constructed with a minimum of possible misunderstandings and adverse reaction.

The final construction of the custom-made questionnaire can now go ahead and decisions made as to whether the audit shall extend to all at a particular level in the organisation, to a sample of the audit population, how large a sample, and so on. The questionnaire, with an accompanying introductory letter and a glossary, is then sent out as agreed. The completed questionnaires are then analysed by computer firstly in general then in specific area terms, the extent of this analysis having been agreed at the contract stage.

Questionnaires can obviously be used as straight alternatives to structured interviews, whatever the approach. However, if used for this purpose there are even more dangers. Pre-determined questions which would have been posed at an interview are written into the questionnaire, such as

- What problems do you encounter in your work?
- Which aspects of your work do you like most?
- Which aspects of your work do you like least?

- What do you feel have been your major accomplishments?
- How could your work be improved?
- What goals do you have?
- What training needs do you feel you have?

It is essential that the questions are open and can be answered by more than a few cryptic words. The problems which relate to such a questionnaire are all those cited as being related to the interview, in addition to the fact that

- there is even less flexibility
- the answers cannot be challenged
- the respondents may answer perfunctorily
- the questionnaire may not be returned.

THE DIARY METHOD

An individual, or group of individuals, is requested to maintain a diary at work over an agreed period of time. The entries in the diary must relate to their activities during the agreed period. Depending on the use which is to be made of the analysis of the diary, either only the activities are noted (or additionally the time involved is shown), or certain categories are selected for noting whenever they occur. At the end of the agreed period the diary entries are analysed and conclusions drawn for immediate use or amalgamation with information obtained by other approaches.

This method has been used very successfully, but to ensure that it is effective, the people completing the diary must be fully committed to the completion since it is easy to forget to enter items or, if you are not a 'diary' sort of person, to fail to complete it over the required period. The diary is also very susceptible to the inclusion of entries which fill it up 'because there should be an entry about that' or 'I'd better put something in for that period, otherwise it will look bad!'

On the positive side, however, diary analyses have shown aspects of work to recur when this was not appreciated, or take up more time than was realised, or to have been given too high a priority.

CRITICAL INCIDENT TECHNIQUE

The critical incident approach can be used with either groups or individuals, both situations requiring similar techniques. The individual is asked to identify and record each day or week an incident or activity which was the most difficult to do that day or week. In this respect, as in the subsequent analysis, it is rather like the diary method, but since it does not require constant or continuous attention it is more likely to be acceptable.

An alternative method of dealing with groups is to use the critical person approach. Here the group is asked to identify a 'bad' manager for whom they have worked and to write down words which describe the aspects which in their view made him 'bad'. The various views are collated to produce a combined description of the areas in which problems can occur. This approach can be considered the negative approach. A similar exercise can then take place but this time identifying the factors which made a 'good' manager they have known – this is the positive side of the analysis.

This latter approach is similar to the performance questionnaire which is a questionnaire in which the respondents discriminate between two statements – one of effective operation, the other of ineffective – applied to a number of skills and attitudes. There is the risk that this type of questionnaire will become lifeless, so respondents are asked to complete it in terms of someone effective they have known, and then somebody ineffective.

BRAINSTORMING

Brainstorming has long been known as an effective problem-solving technique, but it can be readily adapted to produce an analysis of training needs when the analyst has a group of people who are willing to work with him in this way.

Brainstorming has its basis in the lateral thinking approach of creative thinkers such as Edward de Bono. A meeting is organised with the objective of producing as many ideas as possible but without evaluating them at that time. The discussion of any idea generated is banned so as to ensure that free-thinking is not dampened and so that what might appear to be a wild idea may in fact turn out to be perfectly operable.

The group leader, perhaps the analyst in this case, presents the brainstorm topic such as 'The training needs of a newly-appointed supervisor', and asks for ideas. These usually come slowly at first and then more quickly as the group relaxes and enters into the spirit of the exercise. Initially the ideas which emerge are usually traditional but become more radical when the group starts thinking laterally instead of only logically and rationally; they may become very radical towards the end when the members feel they may be throwing in ideas only to make the numbers up. It is often these later ideas which can become the most important, perhaps not as proposed but with modifications.

The list of ideas produced during the brainstorm is later analysed or evaluated by the same or another group, or by the individual whose responsibility it might be to make the decision. The results can be much more extensive and wide-ranging than from many other methods, but it has the disadvantage that the whole process can be lengthy and time-consuming.

MIRRORING

Mirroring is an extension of intergroup, interactive processes which brings problem issues out into the open and produces effective solutions as a result of this openness. In the same way, the technique can be used in evaluation by encouraging the surfacing of negative, ineffective and inappropriate views and attitudes.

One example could be when two or three conflicting groups are brought together and are required to ask the question of each other: 'What do *you* think that *we* think *your* opinion of us is?'

This question asked of, say, the marketing group by the production group might produce the answer: 'We (the marketing group) think that you (the production group) think that we (the marketing group) consider you (the production group) as a bunch of dirty-nailed labourers without any other thoughts . . . (and so on).'

The way is now open for the other group to comment on this view, but without direct threat as all that has been said is what somebody else thinks that you are thinking. Consequently with this once-removed statement there is considerable room for discussion and misconceptions can be clarified so that the real outline of a job and its characteristics can be determined to everybody's satisfaction.

PSYCHOLOGICAL TESTS

The climate favouring the use of psychological tests varies very widely and even when it is highly supportive there are many individuals and organisations who will not even consider their use. The opposite situation applies in times when such approaches are out of favour – many will still want to use them.

Psychological tests are not commonly used in job analysis since they are intended principally to test the person rather than the job. However, because the person has a strong influence on the job in so many cases, particularly in the non-technical types of work, the tests must be an instrument supporting the analysis. The word 'support' is significant as it is in this role that the tests and their results will be most useful – as an aid to other job analysis approaches. One useful approach to which psychological tests can be put in job analysis is in the identification of a person profile for that job. If the people who are performing the job effectively are tested and a common profile emerges, this can then become a profile for the job; a tool which can be particularly useful in selection processes. However, if an individual differs considerably from the common profile, such a difference suggests that it is worth investigating this individual who may have some training needs, training needs which make him different from the profile.

Using psychological tests in job analysis requires caution since even with a reliable and validated test, results are not guaranteed 100 per cent.

4
TECHNIQUES OF ANALYSIS: THE REPERTORY GRID

Within the analysis approaches described in the previous chapter, the ways in which they are used and the methods employed are very varied. In the observational approach the methods can range from simply observing without a plan to a very rigidly structured method. Similarly, the techniques of interviewing can vary considerably. One of these is known as the repertory grid.

AIMS OF THE REPERTORY GRID

The technique of repertory grids for use in interviewing and obtaining views, information and attitudes arose from Kelly's clinical work in 1955 on what are termed the 'personal constructs' of people. Kelly suggested that our minds construct maps of what we see about us in both material and people terms and these maps, which are highly individual in nature, guide our behaviour. From this basis two assumptions are made:

1   If we can identify an individual's 'construct' map there is a strong possibility we can predict his behaviour.

42

2   We may be able to modify an individual's map, and
consequently his behaviour, by some form of training.

There is little quantitative evidence to support these
assumptions but qualitative evidence abounds. As far as the
first assumption is concerned, we know that when we get to
know a person well we also discover 'how they think', and
in most cases we can predict how they will react to a given
situation. Should the second assumption not be true, there
has been considerable time and money wasted training
people to behave differently!

The repertory grid uses the concept of the individual
possession of personal constructs in an interview situation
and from this is determined the individual's views of the
subject. The principal value in the use of the grid compared
with a number of other techniques is that the interviewer
can have a minimal role and consequently the respondent's
views are less susceptible to external contamination.

This technique exposes two aspects of the repertory grid:

Elements are the objects of an individual's thinking and
to which he relates his concepts or values. These elements
may be people – 'an effective manager I know, an ineffective one, an average one' – or they may be objects
or abstract or concrete concepts – 'the repertory grid
technique, the in-depth interview, the psychological test'.
Constructs are the qualities we use to describe the elements
in our personal, individual world. 'He is an effective
manager because he has a humane relationship with his
staff' reflects one personal construct as applied to the
element of a known, assessed effective, manager.

During the repertory grid interview a relatively simple
approach which relates an individual's constructs directly
with the elements is used.

Firstly, the elements are listed and, as suggested earlier,
these usually include a range of effective, ineffective and
average performers, or other elements related to the subject
being investigated.

When these elements have been listed the range of
qualities which the individual uses to describe the elements is

encouraged to emerge and these qualities are rated over the range of elements. From these views a matrix of comparisons is produced, usually with scored ratings for each element against each construct.

Most problems and difficulties occur when all the data has been gathered: it has to be analysed and, as there may be more than fifty items of information or ratings multiplied by the number of individuals involved in the exercise, the problems can be extreme. To aid the analytical process a number of pre-written programs for computer use have been produced and these can certainly speed the production of an end result. Some analysis is possible, however, by manual methods, although this is necessarily time-consuming.

THE REPERTORY GRID IN PRACTICE

Let us use as an example to demonstrate the grid, an analysis of the qualities required in a management trainer, with a view to writing a behavioural job description. In order to obtain a representative view a group of existing management trainers will be used and a group of managers who have undergone a reasonable amount of training. The grid, of course, can be used with an individual if the intention is to analyse that person's views only. The procedure followed is the same whether with groups or with an individual, but the use of groups means that

(a) a greater sample view is obtained
(b) more grids have to be analysed

whereas when the grid is applied to an individual

(a) the results relate to that individual alone
(b) only one grid has to be analysed.

A grid scoring form is used and a typical example of such a form is reproduced as figure 4.1. The number of vertical columns depends on the number of elements used.

The number of horizontal columns is not critical as more than one sheet can be used for the constructs if this should become necessary. In this example, six elements will be used to ensure that everybody knows in sufficient detail the same

REPERTORY GRID SCORING SHEET

	1	2	3	4	5	6	7	8	9	

Figure 4.1

number of people. Nine or more elements are preferable, but this number is not always possible. The process of producing the Repertory Grid can be broken down into nine steps.

Step one. The members of the group identify six management trainers whom they know quite well. If possible, these management trainers should fall into the categories of two effective trainers, two not very effective trainers and two roughly average ones.

Step two. Each member is given six pieces of card or paper on which he writes the names of the people he has identified in step one. These are the elements described earlier. A number can also be added to the card, the number being related to that at the head of the column on the scoring sheet. Alternatively, the name itself can be entered on the scoring sheet as well, as in Figure 4.2.

Step three. Three cards are selected, for example 1, 2 and 3, and each member is asked to identify some aspect related to management training effectiveness which makes two of the three people selected different from the third. As a very simple construct this might be 'fat' for the pair.

The construct word or phrase, in this case 'fat', is written in the top left-hand space of the vertical columns. In the top right-hand space of the vertical columns is written the description of the singleton, the 'odd one out of the three'. In this case it will probably be 'thin'.

This process of obtaining constructs from the three people is continued until no further constructs can be elicited.

Step four. Once the constructs have been elicited and entered on the sheet, the cards are returned to the pile.

Each 'element' person is then given a score of, for example, 1 to 5. A score of 1 or 2 is allocated to those who fit or nearly fit the description in the left-hand column, the column with the description of the pair. Scores of 5 or 4 are allocated to those who fit or nearly fit the description in the right-hand column, the description of the singleton. This completion is shown in Figure 4.2 for one construct.

REPERTORY GRID SCORING SHEET

(Pairs similarity)	JOE	FRED	MARY	HARRY	JEAN	EDDIE				(Singles description)
	1	2	3	4	5	6	7	8	9	
Fat	×1	×5	×2	3	4	1				Thin

Figure 4.2

Step five. A different set of three cards is then selected, say cards 4, 5 and 6 and the process in steps 3 and 4 is repeated, always ensuring that the pairs description is recorded in the left-hand column and a score of 1 or 2 relates to the pairs description and 4 or 5 to the singleton description. A score of 3 is an average or middle-of-the-road score. It helps if at least one 1 and one 5 are allocated – these will usually be from the set of three people for whom the constructs are being elicited.

Step six. Step five is repeated so that the various combinations of the elements can be covered or until the participants run out of constructs to enter.

A suitable series for 6 or 9 elements would be

6 elements	9 elements
1 2 3	1 2 3
4 5 6	4 5 6
1 3 6	7 8 9
2 4 6	1 3 5
1 2 4	2 4 6
3 5 6	3 5 9
2 3 5	4 6 8
1 4 6	1 8 9
and so on	1 2 9
	and so on.

The grid consideration is now complete and the grid scoring sheet of each participant records his views of each element against each construct which has been offered. Obviously much data has been generated and the problem arises of analysing the data. As suggested earlier, the analysis can be produced on the computer, using one of the pre-written programs, but not everybody has recourse to a computer and this may lead to the danger that the Grid approach is ignored or rejected.

However, there is a manual approach which can extract a substantial amount of information from a grid. We can continue our example to see how this is done. Steps 1 to 6 are carried out and part of a possible scoring sheet of one of the participants is shown at Figure 4.3.

REPERTORY GRID SCORING SHEET

	JOE	FRED	MARY	HARRY	JEAN	EDDIE				
	1	2	3	4	5	6	7	8	9	
Run courses with many activities	x 1	x 1	2	4	3	x 5				Most of course consists of lectures
Uses a wide range of aids in lectures	3	2	x 1	x 2	x 5	3				Just talks in lectures
Has an empathy with students	x 1	2	x 2	5	3	x 5				Has a stand-offish approach
Is a swashbuckler in arrangements	3	x 1	4	x 2	x 5	5				Has careful approach to training arrangements
Prefers learner-centred training	x 1	4	x 5	x 2	3	5				Prefers tutor centred training
Is knowledgeable over a wide range of methods	2	x 1	3	3	x 5	x 2				Limited knowledge of methods
Has an easy articulation	x 1	x 2	3	x 5	4	3				Explanations are unclear
Always presents a good professional appearance	x 1	x 5	x 2	3	1	5				Can often be over-casually dressed
Prefers to work unaided	1	3	2	x 1	x 3	x 5				Always wants tutor support
Activist	x 2	x 1	3	4	x 5	3				Reflector
Effective	1	1	2	3	4	5				Ineffective
(reversed scores)	5	5	4	3	2	1				

Figure 4.3

In this case the constructs are those related to the behavioural aspects of the management trainer. The person conducting the exercise must be careful not to contaminate the results by suggesting constructs – these must be the result of the thoughts of the individual participants and expressed in their own words. However, the constructs must be understandable, particularly if a number of people are involved, so the analyst can help to clarify the wording of the construct – without changing its meaning.

Once the constructs have been listed against the elements as far as is possible or desirable, the grid results can be scored to produce a ready to use analysis.

Step seven. In this example we are considering the behavioural aspects of a management trainer related to his overall effectiveness, therefore at the end of the grid the participants are asked to rate the elements in a single, given construct over a scale effective to ineffective. This rating is shown at the bottom of Figure 4.3.

The scoring for overall effectiveness can then be compared with individual aspects to highlight differences and provide effectiveness indicators. In order that a check on scoring can be made the overall effectiveness scores are reversed. This reversed rating is also shown at the bottom of Figure 4.3.

Step eight. The scorings for each construct line are obtained by producing and noting the difference for each element against the overall effectiveness figures. For example, for the first construct we find

Runs courses with many activities	$1\,_4^-$	$1\,_4^-$	$2\,_2^-$	4_1^1	3_1^1	$5\,_4^-$	$_{16R}^2$	Most of course consists of lectures.

Effective	1	1	2	3	4	5	Ineffective
Effective reversed	5	5	4	3	2	1	Ineffective reversed

The larger figures are the original scorings, the small figures the difference (it doesn't matter whether + or −) between these scorings and the effectiveness ratings, both direct and

REPERTORY GRID SCORING SHEET

	JOE 1	FRED 2	MARY 3	HARRY 4	JEAN 5	EDDIE 6	7	8	9		
Run courses with many activities	x^- 1_4	x^- 1_4	$-$ 2_2	1 4_1	1 3_1	x^- 5_4				Most of course consists of lectures	2 R16
Uses a wide range of aids in lectures	2 3_2	1 2_3	x^1 1_3	x^1 2_1	x^1 5_3	2 3_2				Just talks in lectures	8 R14
Has an empathy with students	x^- 1_4	1 2_3	x^- 2_2	3 5_2	1 3_1	x^- 5_4				Has a stand-offish approach	5 R16
Is a swashbuckler in arrangements	2 3_2	x^- 1_4	2 4_-	x^1 2_1	x^3 5_3	$-$ 5_4				Has careful approach to training arrangements	8 R14
Prefers learner-centred training	x^- 1_4	3 4_1	x^3 5_1	x^1 2_1	1 3_1	$-$ 5_4				Prefers tutor centred training	8 R12
Is knowledgeable over a wide range of methods	1 2_3	x^- 1_4	1 3_1	$-$ 3_-	x^1 5_3	x^3 2_1				Limited knowledge of methods	6 R12
Has an easy articulation	x^- 1_4	x^1 2_3	1 3_1	x^2 5_2	$-$ 4_2	2 3_2				Explanations are unclear	6 R14
Always presents a good professional appearance	x^- 1_4	x^4 5_-	x^- 2_2	$-$ 3_-	3 1_1	$-$ 5_5				Can often be over-casually dressed	7 R11
Prefers to work unaided	$-$ 1_4	2 3_2	$-$ 2_2	x^2 1_2	x^1 3_1	x^- 5_4				Always wants tutor support	5 R15
Activist	x^1 2_3	x^- 1_4	1 3_1	1 4_1	x^1 5_3	2 3_2				Reflector	6 R14
Effective	1	1	2	3	4	5				Ineffective	
(reversed scores)	5	5	4	3	2	1					
~~internally~~ Trained externally	x^- 1_4	x^1 2_3	x^3 5_1	2 5_2	3 1_1	4 1_-				Trained ~~externally~~ internally	13 R11

Figure 4.4

reversed. The direct differences are the upper, smaller figures and the reversed differences the lower, smaller figures. The differences have been added to the scoring sheet and are included in Figure 4.4.

If the total scores for a construct show the reversed score difference to be smaller than the direct, effective score, the construct descriptions should be reversed. An example of this is shown at the bottom of Figure 4.4.

Step nine. We are now in a position to analyse the various constructs on the basis of the lower the score, the more significant is that aspect in the effectiveness ranking, at least in the view of the person completing the grid. From the example used, the aspects which go towards the behavioural skills of a management trainer, in descending order of effectiveness, are

Runs courses with many activities	2	
Has empathy with students	5	
Prefers to work unaided	5	More
Is an activist	6	effective
Articulates easily	6	aspects
Is knowledgeable over a wide range of methods	6	
Always presents a good professional appearance	7	
Is a swashbuckler in arrangements	8	
		Less
Prefers learner-centred training	8	effective
Uses a wide range of methods	8	aspects.
Trained externally	11	

Of course these are the views of only one individual and may, on their own, represent an extreme view. If, however, as large a group as possible is asked to complete the Grid, a more representative picture should emerge, even if this is based on a majority view. When analysing the views of a large number of people, it may be useful to sort out the views into tops and tails – say the four lowest scoring and the four highest – from each participant. Although different words may have been used by different people, the same general views can usually be expressed in one category, but beware of categorising with one's own bias in view. At least two other people can be brought into this process to avoid contamination of the categorisation, either on a discussive basis to decide on overlapping statements or as independent categorisers. The top set of categories can then be stated as the most effective aspects necessary.

Even the widest approach in this way can still introduce bias – namely that of the trainers themselves who may see the role of the trainer in a completely different way from the people they train. So, in order to reflect these possibly different views the exercise can be repeated with a group of people who are the normal training population of the trainers concerned. The two final lists can then be compared to identify any different views and to take these into account in the final analysis.

INTERVIEWER INTERVENTION

The procedure above describes the role of the analyst as a provider of a description of the method and pieces of paper; a monitor of the correct operation of the process; and as the subsequent principal analyst, although steps 7, 8 and 9 can be performed by the grid participants themselves. Any further intrusion, particularly in suggesting constructs, will contaminate the exercise. Obviously the Grid results can be analysed in much greater depth than suggested in the analysis described above, but it will be in such an extension that the computer will become necessary.

The practical intervention of the analyst, although always attempting to avoid contamination, may consist of the selection of element headings for consideration. The analyst may also *help* the participant to produce constructs or clarify them by asking questions designed to aid the individual, but must never suggest constructs except the final comparison one ranging from effectiveness to ineffectiveness.

PROBLEMS OF THE REPERTORY GRID

The grid technique is obviously not without problems – few techniques are – and contamination by the analyst as described can certainly be a possible problem, particularly when the participants are having difficulty in providing constructs.

Time is a particularly significant problem since the completion of the grid is not always straightforward. The larger and therefore more reliable the grid, the longer it takes to complete and the greater the risk of loss of interest on the part of the completer. If the completer is involved in all the stages the risk of loss of interest will be minimised, but with a resultant increase in time involvement. Even a relatively simple grid as used in the example will take the major part of an hour to set up and complete the constructs. The scoring then has to be completed, and the simple analysis. From start to finish the time necessary can range between a minimum of an hour to more than two hours.

If there are a number of interviewees involved, more time will be needed and certainly more time will be necessary for analysis. The location of interviewees is linked with time. The problems associated with location are eased if those people who have to be interviewed are all together in one place. If they are scattered throughout the country obvious problems of time, availability, travelling and cost are introduced.

An initial problem of definition, particularly in the setting and wording of the objectives and the relevancy of the elements to these objectives, can negate the remainder of the exercise. Smith and Ashton cite the case of a list of dog vaccines used as elements in an analysis which involved vets. Unfortunately the vets had insufficient knowledge of all the vaccines put forward as elements and the construction of the grid was very difficult as a result. It may therefore be necessary to restrict to some extent the range of elements and constructs used. However, if too much control is imposed, the results can be unreliable through contamination or reaction by those participating. If there is no control, the choices made by the participants can be so wide and individually centred that any comparisons are impossible.

In spite of the problems suggested in the use of the repertory grid technique, particularly in the eliciting of constructs, there can be little doubt that it is a method which has a low risk of contamination by the views, values and attitudes of the interviewer. It is a very time-consuming method and consequently there is a risk that the individuals may lose interest during the grid construction. A particular, common problem is the difficulty of finding constructs. This can be caused by the recommended method of using three elements and determining differences between two of them compared with the third. It is often difficult to find an aspect which is common to only two of the elements. Sometimes there can be a difference between two of the elements which cannot be identified with the third element. I have discovered through experience that the problem is solved by asking the participant to produce comparisons between two elements. After all the basic principle of eliciting constructs is to obtain comparisons between elements: if the participants can produce constructs by producing comparison between two elements, the objective has been achieved.

5
TECHNIQUESOF
ANALYSIS:
OBSERVATIONAL
METHODS

The repertory grid described in the last chapter involved directly those people performing or receiving the work under consideration, and asked them to do something practical, even to the stage of the final analysis. However, there are other approaches which exclude the direct involvement of the people being analysed and require only the involvement of the analyst. These approaches are concerned with job analysis by observation and provide objective and quantitative assessments. The various approaches can be classified roughly as process observation and behavioural observation. Process observation is strictly concerned with what is done in the job in functional terms such as turning a tap, picking up a pen and so on. Behaviour observation is interested in what is said, how it is said, the manner of the person and so on.

PROCESS OBSERVATION

Most jobs or tasks involve the practitioner in doing something which is visible to the observer, either all the time or most of the time. The observation of these practical activities is called process observation and gives us most of our information about most jobs.

Process observation can range from simple, unstructured work observation to highly sophisticated approaches. It exists even in the situation where Auntie Flo, on a coach trip to a pottery works, having watched the potter at his task for a while, turns to Auntie Mabel and says 'I didn't realise that his job was so complicated!'

At the other end of the spectrum is someone such as the work study expert who observes the performance of a job against a check list of all the tasks to be performed. He notes such things as which tasks are or are not performed, how often they are performed, how long each operation and task takes and so on. The results are then analysed to identify superfluous operations, and solutions are offered to tasks which take too long to perform. These observations and analyses are timed within seconds and fractions of seconds.

The more commonly practised approaches lie between Auntie Flo and the work study expert approach and involve a relatively simple observational tool. This process or job content observation sheet lists the range of specific tasks involved in a job or sub-tasks in a task. The observer watches the worker and logs a scoring mark on the sheet each time a task or sub-task is performed. For example, if we are observing the activities of the hotel receptionist, we are aware from the job specification or some previous observation, that a range of tasks are performed within the job. These tasks, such as answering the telephone, responding to customer enquiries, issuing receipts, are listed and scored as the receptionist performs the task. At the end of the observational period or periods, the observation sheets are analysed and this analysis can determine how often each task is performed, at which time of the day are the tasks performed most, and so on. An example process observation sheet is shown at Figure 5.1.

BEHAVIOUR OBSERVATION

The methods of behaviour observation have many similarities with those of process observation, which is natural since

Hotel Receptionist

Time periods

						TOTAL

Answers telephone

Makes telephone call – internal

– external

Answers customer enquiry – rooms

– meals

– other

Figure 5.1   Process/content analysis

it is the observation of someone performing an activity. But on this occasion the interest lies in the behaviour of the performer rather than the practical functions of the job.

Behaviour observation is based on the selection of categories of behaviour which may or may not be involved in the job, observation of the incidence of these behaviours and an annotation of this incidence and subsequent analysis of these annotations. The selection of the behaviour categories is relatively simple if it is known beforehand which behaviours are needed to perform the job and which behaviours are not. If, however, the observation is general in its approach or the analysis is investigatory, the range of behaviours chosen may have to be extensive. The criteria for the selection of the behaviour categories will relate to the type of operation being observed and the reasons for the observation. If the activity is that of a group leader or a chairman, the categories will be different from those required in the observation of a one-to-one interview.

Let us use the example of an appraisal interview which we wish to analyse by behaviour observation. We are generally aware of the behaviours used in such an activity, but we wish to analyse how often each behaviour occurs and relate this to the effectiveness of the interviewer.

BEHAVIOUR CATEGORIES

We must first decide which behaviours to observe and analyse. The interviewer will naturally have to ask questions, give information, make suggestions, support or disagree with the interviewee, and so on. Some of the categories can be subdivided in order to define more closely the behaviour. For example, questioning can be divided into various forms such as closed, multiple, and leading. Similarly proposals or suggestions can be subdivided into effective and ineffective proposals, content and procedure proposals, suggestions as opposed to proposals and so on.

The range of categories can also be determined from previous observations of interviews in which the interview is analysed firstly in terms of the categories used and how frequently they occur.

The final decision on the number of categories is based on the physical restrictions of the observer: how experienced the observer is in conducting analyses and how many categories can be controlled to a reasonable level of accuracy of observation. In general, the more experienced the observer, the greater the number of categories can be observed.

A basic list of categories would probably consist of

- asking questions
- giving information
- suggesting/proposing
- supporting
- disagreeing
- interrupting
- other behaviours

This list is capable of giving a reasonable analysis of an interaction yet is short enough to be coped with by a relatively inexperienced observer. But most experienced observers should be capable of handling more categories, particularly as the interaction involves the observation of two people only, or even one if the interviewer alone is being observed. This is quite different from observing a group in which an observer has to score the category contributions of a number of people.

A realistic list of categories under these circumstances could consist of

- suggesting/proposing
- open questions
- closed questions
- multiple questions
- leading questions
- reflections
- giving information
- disagreeing (without reasons stated)
- disagreeing (with reasons stated)
- testing understanding
- summarising
- open

- supporting
- attacking/blocking
- interrupting

DEFINITIONS OF CATEGORIES

Most of these categories are straightforward in their meaning, but some have definitions which extend their usefulness. It is obviously essential that the observer understands completely the definitions of the categories so that there can be no confusion. This requirement also demands that the categories themselves must be clear and capable of unequivocable definition, are capable of identification, are sufficiently different from each other to warrant a separate category, and are meaningful.

Suggesting/Proposing. These are the ideas put forward for discussion or agreement leading to a positive end result of the interaction. They can take various forms and will range from ideas put forward for consideration to directives to perform in a particular way. Examples of this range can be
'I suggest that we . . . .'
'I propose we do . . . '
'Let's do . . . '
'How do you feel if we . . . '
'I think your approach should be . . . '
'What did you think of the event?'

Open questions. These questions are usually prefaced by 'what?' 'why?' 'how?' and leave the way open to the respondent to give detailed answers limited only by the depth which he is willing to disclose. Such a question might be: 'What did you think of the event?'

Closed questions. These can be answered by a simple 'yes' or 'no' and have to be followed up to elicit fuller information. A question such as: 'Did you enjoy that event?' might lead to the answer 'No', which in turn would lead to the further question 'Why did you not enjoy it?' The eventual information could usually have been obtained by asking an open question in the first place, thus saving a number of questions. However, there are occasions when a closed question is the appropriate approach.

Multiple questions. Unless the respondent has a particularly astute mind and can handle three or more questions at the same time and will answer them all unprompted, the multiple question is dangerous. If one asks: 'Well now, I want to get your views on the present situation, so can you tell me what you think is happening with x. Of course, this has an effect on conditions in y. What do you think of this effect? And I see you have recently come back from z. What were things like there?' Assuming the respondent has not been completely confused, he is most likely to answer only the last question, as that was the last he heard. He will select this area to answer because it was the last subject, and also because it is a question which poses the least threat. If you need to know the answer to all three subjects, pose them as three separate questions.

Leading questions. Whether the intention is deliberate or not, a question from a boss to a subordinate couched in the terms: 'Don't you feel it is time we . . . ?' will tell the subordinate firstly that the *boss* feels that it is time and secondly that the boss feels that *the subordinate* should also feel that it is time. Of course the subordinate can ignore the leading implications, treating the question as a closed one and answering 'yes' or 'no' – (the latter perhaps at his peril!)

Reflections. These are restatements of what the speaker has just said, usually made with the intention of encouraging him to continue with that topic. 'You feel that it is time that you did something about . . . ', expressed as a statement not as a question is such a category.

Giving information is the category used to describe statements offering either information or views, thoughts or opinions, feelings or attitudes.

Disagreeing (without reasons stated) as a category is used to denote bald, blunt statements of disagreement such as 'I disagree', 'No, I don't agree with that' or 'No, I can't go along with that'. The disagreement is stated without reasons being given. It can elicit a variety of responses ranging from 'Why do you disagree?' through non-reaction to 'Who do you think you are to disagree with me!'.

Disagreeing (with reasons stated) is much more likely to produce a positive response since, although the disagreement is still there, the basis for it is explained.

Testing understanding is a category in which one interactor questions whether what has been said by the other person has been understood correctly. 'If I got it correctly, you feel that you . . . Is that right?'

Summarising. This is the collective statement usually, although not always, made by the chairman or leader, which summarises what has been discussed and what has been agreed during the interaction up to that particular stage. Interim summaries are valuable so that all parties are clear about progress through the various stages, with a summary at the end to tie everything together. A summary can, of course, occur at the beginning of an interaction if it is the continuance of a previous meeting: in this case it is concerned with recounting the stage reached by the previous meeting.

Open. An open contribution is made when an error or mistake is admitted or regret is expressed, such as 'I'm sorry. That was my mistake. I should have noticed it in the report.'

Supporting. This category of behaviour occurs when an overt, direct, verbal statement is made supporting another person's views, feelings, opinions, ideas or proposals. It can take the simple form of 'I agree' or 'Yes, I'll go along with that', or can be a long statement repeating what has just been said, but in different words.

Attacking/Blocking. These two categories are put together as they are both negative rather than supportive. The 'attacking' category is used when the statement is openly aggressive or abusive and has an emotional context. For example 'I might have expected *you* to suggest that' will readily be seen as an attack on the proposer, eliciting the likely response of an equally attacking retort, and so on along the attack/defend spiral.

Blocking occurs when a contribution is made which adds nothing of positive value to the interaction. The classical block is 'Oh, we're just going around in circles'. This may indeed be true, but stating it so bluntly only halts the interaction. Someone else then has to take a positive step to move the interaction forward.

Interrupting. When one or more persons interrupt a speaker while he is speaking, very clear messages are being given which are important indicators of the effectiveness of the interaction. Among other things, the interrupter is saying to the speaker

'Shut up'

'I'm not listening to what you are saying'

'What I have to say is more important than what you are saying'.

BEHAVIOUR OBSERVATION FORMS

If we wish to observe an interaction in detail and make notes on it, the last thing we want is a complicated observation instrument. Our observation form must be as simple as possible yet be capable of producing results suitable for analysis.

Figure 5.2 illustrates a useful form of observational and analytical instrument which can be used to observe the appraisal interview we are using as an example. It lists the fifteen categories previously defined, each category occupying a horizontal row, with vertical columns for the participants.

	INT'ER	INT'EE	TOTAL
Suggesting/Proposing			
Open questions			
Closed questions			
Multiple questions			
Leading questions			
Reflecting			
Giving Information			
Disagreeing without reasons			
Disagreeing with reasons			
Testing Understanding			
Summarising			
Supporting			
Open			
Attacking/Blocking			
Interrupting			
TOTALS			

Figure 5.2 Behaviour observation form

As the interaction proceeds, a stroke is placed in the column relating to the person making the contribution, and against the identified category of that contribution. Figure 5.2 shows that the interviewer made the first contribution of the interaction by describing to the interviewee the form that the interview would take. This is shown by a stroke against the category 'giving information'.

More strokes are added as each participant makes a contribution and the completed observation sheet appears in Figure 5.3.

ANALYSIS OF THE INTERACTION

The analytical observational record of the appraisal interview shown in Figure 5.3 demonstrates the behaviour pattern of a not very effective interviewer. It can be seen from the number of proposals made by the interviewer and the lack of proposals made by the interviewee that the interview took a very prescriptive line. This pattern is reflected throughout the record of the interview and it is obvious that the event was far from being an effective appraisal. The record shows that the majority of contributions have been made by the interviewer stating his own opinions, asking closed questions, disagreeing and other negative behaviour. The effects of this approach by the interviewer can be seen in the contributions of the interviewee. The interviewee offers little information and is forced to disagree with the interviewer by interrupting frequently when the interviewer was talking.

Neil Rackham and Terry Morgan have undertaken research into appraisal interview behaviour by using behaviour analysis to assess effective behaviours. In order to examine the behaviour of expert appraisers it was first necessary to identify criteria for effectiveness. The criteria identified included whether the appraisees judged the interviews to have been worthwhile and useful; whether the appraisee's performance improved following the interview; and whether there was effective action by the interviewer following the interview. Using these criteria, 117 appraisers were judged as 'expert' and a further sixty-one were

	INT'ER	INT'EE	TOTAL
Suggesting/Proposing	7	1	8
Open questions	2	5	7
Closed questions	18	5	23
Multiple questions	9	–	9
Leading questions	12	–	12
Reflecting	–	–	–
Giving Information	28	5	33
Disagreeing without reasons	2	1	3
Disagreeing with reasons	14	14	28
Testing Understanding	–	–	–
Summarising	1	–	1
Supporting	1	1	2
Open	–	–	–
Attacking/Blocking	8	6	14
Interrupting	8	18	26
TOTALS	110	56	166

Figure 5.3 Behaviour observation form completed

considered on a random choice basis and classified as 'average'. The expert group was eventually reduced to ninety-three, sixty-one of whom produced two tapes each of appraisal interviews they had conducted, and thirty-two of whom who produced one tape each, resulting in a total of 154 interviews.

On analysis these interviews produced a behaviour pattern which showed significant differences between expert and average appraisers. This information is shown in the following table:

| | % of total behaviour | |
	Expert appraisers	Average appraisers
Proposing	8.1	16.2
Building	4.7	1.8
Supporting	11.7	8.3
Disagreeing	7.2	6.8
Defending/ Attacking	0.2	1.3
Testing understanding	8.3	3.1
Summarising	6.4	2.3
Seeking information	15.1	12.7
Seeking proposals/ solutions	6.4	2.0
Giving internal information	14.9	12.0
Giving external information	17.0	33.5

(Reproduced from *Behaviour Analysis in Training* by Neil Rackham and Terry Morgan, (McGraw-Hill, 1977) by kind permission of the authors.)

Behaviour analysis is probably one of the most objective methods of observation and analysis and has a wide and varied use. Observational research with this base has identified a number of appropriate approaches defined in behaviour categories. This research data can thus be compared with the results of other observations and the necessary conclusions made. It will be seen later that behavioural observation and analysis can be introduced at the initial analysis stage, during training events to determine continuous change, and at the end of the training to identify any terminal change from the initial state.

6
NOW WE'RE READY TO TRAIN

Preceding chapters have suggested that it is of little value even to consider validation or evaluation if the initial groundwork has not been laid in order to determine the extent of the change, or training, necessary.

It has also been suggested that, if it has not already been obtained, data as quantitative as possible should be determined about

(a) what the job requires in terms of knowledge, skills and attitudes
(b) what knowledge, skills and attitude levels are currently possessed by the potential training population.

From this data the gap between a and b should be determined: the level of existing knowledge, skills and attitude produces the training need. The information required in a and b above can be obtained in a number of ways such as through job descriptions, job analysis, job specification and job/task observation.

By this stage the needs of an individual or group should be clear, and from what level they need to start. If at the end of the training event, or subsequently, new levels of knowledge, skill or attitude are found to be higher than at the start, the training is validated and the organisation will be receiving some benefit. At least one can make this *assumption* and in some cases it must be an assumption.

If the training need and the existing level are determined both immediately before the training event and immediately afterward, there can be little doubt about the role played by the training. But assessment before the training event is not always possible and the trainer is always more interested in the real effect of the training: whether the learner has changed sufficiently to put the learning into practice. This can only be assessed some time after the training. Obviously with delays possible both before and after the training, contamination of an assessment of the effect of training can occur. It may be that the learner would have learned without the infusion of training!

CONTROL GROUPS

One approach which attempts to answer this criticism is the use of what are known as control groups; groups which are as similar as possible to the group which is being trained. Ideally they must be a complete match in terms of job, age, experience, skill level, education, intelligence and so on. It is the realistic application of this matching which presents the greatest difficulty in the use of control groups: matching is simple to state in theory but difficult to put into practice, and a number of subjective assessments may have to be made.

In the simplest control group approach where one control group is compared with the training group, the control group receives no training but is given the pre- and post-training tasks as if the members had undergone the training. The training group, of course, has the training and the pre- and post-training testing.

The use of control systems involving more than one control group is possible, and in many ways desirable, since the greater the number of control groups the more objectively valid will be the measurement of change or no change. However, the larger the number of control groups, the greater the administrative problems.

It is essential that any pre- or post-training tests are administered to a control group using exactly the same tests as those given to a training group, and under consistent and similar conditions, preferably at the same time. As suggested earlier the results must be treated with some care. If the non-training group shows a similar change over the period to that of the training group, serious doubts must be expressed about whether the training is necessary. If the non-training group, however, shows no change whereas there is substantial change within the training group, this supports the view that the change has been due to the training. If the result lies some way between these two extremes, the trainer must question whether all the training is necessary.

The pre-training stages and steps are followed by the training itself. Descriptions of the many approaches possible are provided in many of the books and articles listed in the bibliography. However, aspects of validation impinge on the early stages of a training event: in fact they continue through and beyond the training to such an extent that it is difficult to separate them.

INITIAL ASSESSMENTS

Sometimes it is necessary to make assessments at the start of a training event. This is essential if for some reason, as happens in so many cases, there has been no pre-training investigation. At the very least the trainer requires to know the level of the participants in order that he can adjust the training to this level. Unless pre-training assessments have been made, the starting level needs to be determined in order to assess any change following the training. Consequently there is a wide range of approaches and many of the methods are also those in use at other stages of validation. The more common approaches used at this stage are:

Knowledge/Skill assessment
Knowledge tests   — Open answer
                                  Binary choice
                                  Multiple choice
                                  Short answer
                                  True/false choice
Skill/Knowledge self-assessment
Skill determination.

KNOWLEDGE/SKILL ASSESSMENT

This approach has obvious limitations, but it can be useful
to the trainer if no pre-training information is available,
since it can
  — warn him of deficiencies in the training group
  — warn him of problems in the training group
  — suggest the range of knowledge/skill/attitude of the
     group.

Most training events open with a session during which the
participants introduce themselves. Usually the introductions
are very superficial with names, locations, jobs and career
histories being given. This type of information is not in
itself particularly helpful, but at least the session acts as an
ice-breaker by giving each trainee an opportunity to start
talking – sometimes it is unfortunately the only time some
individuals speak! The value and use of this form of
introduction can be increased by controlling the content of
the introduction.

For example, at the start of a course concerned with job
appraisal reviews (JAR), the participants could be asked to
introduce themselves in terms of

Name
Location
Number of staff on whom they report
Experience of JAR – types, numbers, etc.
Problems experienced or envisaged
Personal objectives for the course

Part of these comments will be subjective, but they will at least offer some starting material relevant to the training. Notes should be taken of the information so that comparisons can be produced at the end of the course, particularly relating to problems and their resolution, and the satisfaction of the personal objectives of each individual. If these objectives are relevant to the training and have not been satisfied by the end of the course, the training has obviously not been valid for that individual.

This purely oral expression of needs can be extended by having the participants write down their personal objectives and the problem areas they would like to see covered during the training. These written aims, either retained as a personal document or posted up round the walls of the training room, can serve as the basis of a partial validation discussion at or near the end of the course. Have the personal objectives been satisfied? If not, can action be taken now or can plans be made to do something about unresolved problems?

KNOWLEDGE TESTS

At the start of a training course the participants, unless they are completely new entrants to the occupation or industry, will each possess some knowledge. If this knowledge is tested at this early stage, it will enable the trainer to

(a) assess the general level of the group and pitch the training level accordingly
(b) provide the information which will be compared with a later test to determine the changes which have taken place.

Open answer. The most widely known test approach is the examination question approach which sets a question to determine the amount of knowledge possessed. This knowledge is shown in the reply to the question. The problem of this approach is that the answer, which can be expressed in a variety of ways, has to be assessed or even interpreted. The format of the question determines the generality of the answer. A typical question would be 'Compare in as many ways as you can the . . . and the . . . ' Formulating questions requires considerable skill as well as knowledge on the part of the tester, and enough time to complete the assessment and interpretation if a comprehensive examination is to be set.

Binary choice. The knowledge element can be tested by methods which do not require as much time and staff resources as the full examination method. One method is to pose questions related to the subject under consideration and supply alternative answers from which a choice can be made. The selection answers may consist of simple YES or NO, if this is all the question demands, or some short phrases. Examples of these approaches would be:

	(Delete inappropriate answer.)
1. Does your company offer annual job appraisal reviews?	Yes/No
2. To whom would you look for your annual job appraisal review?	Your boss/Your boss's boss?

This approach has the obvious advantage of simplicity and ease, not only in the answers but also in the assessment of the correctness of the answers. However, this very simplicity must limit the approach to some extent since the ability to simplify accurately demands excellent knowledge on the part of the subject and the ability to phrase unambiguous questions on the part of the test constructor. For example, if you were completing the answer to the *yes/no* question posed above, how would you interpret the word 'offer'?

There are a number of rules which must be followed in the construction of binary selection tests and many of these rules apply to other questionnaires. Two important rules are:

(a) The question must consist only of one question and that question must be clear to the reader so that it does not have to be puzzled over for its meaning, otherwise the person being tested may be confused. The intention is to test the knowledge of the person, not to test their ability to interpret ambiguity.

(b) One of the answers given in the alternative answer approach must be correct and there must be no doubt or ambiguity about it as the correct or true answer.

The advantage of this approach is that it is simple to administer and simple for the trainee to understand. It is also speedy in operation. The questions and answers have to be carefully selected if they are not to be too obvious or too unclear. The principal problem is that because there is a choice between two answers only, the trainee may be tempted to guess his answer and he has a fifty-fifty chance of each answer being correct. There will be a diminution of this effect based on the laws of probability, but whatever the statistical basis, the validity of the test could be reduced in the mind of the person tested in addition to the tester.

True/False choice. A similar binary choice test prone to the same probability errors is the True/False test in which the trainee is asked to score a statement in either of these states. For example,

The machine operator only is allowed to press the stop button.	True/False?

Although this test appears simple, as in the case of the Yes/No test it is most difficult to construct and administer since most statements require considerable qualification to ensure that they are clear. The criticism can also be levelled that Yes/No, True/False, or the alternative answers approaches give no reasons 'why'.

Multiple choice. One way of avoiding some of the problems cited above is to extend the range of answers from which the choice has to be made. This approach is often used in television quiz programmes, and a 'silly' answer is frequently included in the list of options. The difference between the multiple and the binary choice approach is that three or more possible answers are provided, usually up to a maximum of 5. For example,

The Job Appraisal Review interview is:
1. Mandatory
2. Voluntary for all staff up to age 60
3. Voluntary for all staff

In this questionnaire the responder has to choose from the answers offered and either tick the selected answer, or ring the number of the chosen answer. The greater the number of optional answers offered, the less chance there is of random selection producing a high score, as is the situation in the binary choice. However, the multiple choice approach is much more difficult to construct because of the need to produce a wide range of optional, incorrect answers.

One variation of the multiple choice approach is given in the example above. It can be described as the incomplete answer test as the stem of the test is completed by one of the answers – 'The Job Appraisal Review interview is voluntary for all staff'.

An alternative is to pose the stem as a question rather than an incomplete statement. For example,

What are the recommended tyre pressures for a Zucat 327?
(a) 28 lbf/in^2 front and rear
(b) 30 lbf/in^2 front and rear
(c) 28 lbf/in^2 front, 30 lbf/in^2 rear
(d) 30 lbf/in^2 front, 28 lbf/in^2 rear
(e) 40 lbf/in^2 front and rear

One variation which is often used, more to establish attitudes based on knowledge and experience rather than to obtain correct answers, is a multiple choice in which the tester has a preferred answer in mind. The other answers are not wrong, only less preferred by the tester, the organisation, research or some other body. For example,

Practical practice interviews are best performed with
(a)   Real-life case studies
(b)   Case studies based on real-life
(c)   Constructed case studies for the interviewer only
(d)   Constructed case studies for the interviewee only.

Obviously in a test such as this it has to be made clear by the tester that the best or preferred answer is required of the responders.

Short answer. Similar in many ways to the binary and multiple choice answer tests is the one which requires the respondent to write a short answer rather than select one from a provided list. This approach is more difficult for the respondent who has to search for not only the answer, but also the words with which to phrase it. For example 'The minimum stopping distance for a car travelling at 40 mph in dry conditions is . . . '

This short answer approach is probably the most effective of the knowledge tests as it is the one which, apart from the full examination approach, requires the respondent, without help from optional answers, to demonstrate his knowledge or lack of it. It also requires considerable work on the part of the tester who has to construct the questions in such a way that they are clear and unambiguous.

SKILLS ASSESSMENT

The assessment of initial skills is often more difficult than straightforward knowledge testing, both for the tester and the tested. Most of us are quite used to written tests of our knowledge, but fewer have been exposed to tests of our skills. This is particularly so in the case of the less practical skills.

It is relatively straightforward to test the practical skills at the start of a training event, in order to assess the initial skill level. Such skills might be the ability to perform a manual task, or one requiring technical skills, the completion of a written task for which there is a recognised structure, or the technical performance of an oral task which allows no personal latitude. These skills can include the operation of an automatic machine, the setting of a complicated machine, correct ledger entries, making clear accurate announcements, and so on. Specific direct tests related to the necessary skills can be set, observed and assessed.

However, many skills, particularly those at management level, are more difficult to test and assess, and any initial assessment must be necessarily much more subjective if the individuals have not been observed *in situ*. It may be suggested that if any attempt at validation has to rely on a subjective assessment, the assessment has little value. But it has been noted earlier that in spite of any difficulties it is always worth trying to produce *some* assessment rather than none at all. Also, there are other validation approaches, even though themselves subjective, which may support the initial assessment.

The approach in circumstances such as this is to have a questionnaire completed by the participants themselves at the start of the training event, a questionnaire related to the training content. In this questionnaire the individuals are asked to rate on a scale how effective they think they are in a number of aspects which will be included in the training event.

Semantic Differential Questionnaire. One common type of questionnaire is based on a semantic differential and in a questionnaire of this nature the participants are asked to rate the aspects on a scale between opposites. For example, a questionnaire for people attending a meetings' management course could include such items as

Preparation of agenda
Skilled |___|___|___| ✓ |___|___|___| Unskilled

Control of meetings
Well |___|___|___|___| ✓ |___|___| Badly

Handling of difficult members
Well |___|___|___|___|___| ✓ |___| Badly

Use of summaries
Frequent |___| ✓ |___|___|___|___|___| Rare
Complete |___|___| ✓ |___|___|___|___| Incomplete
Fully accurate |___|___| ✓ |___|___|___|___| Inaccurate

and so on.

Each individual will complete a questionnaire of this nature and the questionnaire can be held until the end of the course and used for assessment, whether this might be tutor-based or learner-based. It can also be used immediately as a discussion base to start the training course by bringing into the open the different views of the course participants about the levels of their skills.

The semantic differential assessment method requires the individual to make a subjective assessment of his skill using scale divisions ranging from a minimum of three divisions to as many as the trainer feels the individual can handle: a scale with six or seven divisions is about the norm. A mark is placed in the space on the scale which represents the level at which the person feels they are, relative to the descriptions at each end of the scale with the shades in between. There is considerable discussion in scale questionnaire circles as to whether an odd or an even number of divisions is the most effective. If an odd number is chosen, say seven, then there will be a mid division which will at best be treated as the 'average' division and at worst a safe marking which can be given without having to make a real decision. The even division of, for example six, means that the assessor has to be positive in the assessment when away from the extremes, and mark a division on either side of the middle line showing 'satisfactory plus' or 'satisfactory minus'.

Thurstone Scale. One way to avoid the problems of allocating a numerical weighting to a subjective view is to use a Thurstone Scale. This presents the individual with a number of statements related to the training event and requires either agreement or disagreement with each statement. A variation of this approach, which most people seem to prefer, is for the individual to state whether there is agreement or more agreement than disagreement, or disagreement or more disagreement than agreement. This does away with the need to have a choice between the extremes of agreement or disagreement only.

A questionnaire in this form might require answers in the form of: A = You agree or agree more than you disagree; D = You disagree or disagree more than you agree.

1	A manager's first responsibility is the care of his staff	D	A
2	A manager must be able to do all the jobs of his staff	D	A
3	A manager is closer to his staff than to his manager	D	A

The principal advantage of this type of scale is that specific items which require answers can be included in the list and consequently the scale can be used extensively. The tester must, however, be prepared for comments from the group completing the questionnaire who may be attempting to rationalise or defend their answers and who say that

- various interpretations can be placed on the wording of the statement
- they could not be so definite about agreeing or disagreeing, even when taking into account the broad definitions of A and D.

The first objection can in fact be used by a trainer to make the group discuss fully what a question means to all of them before they answer. The second objection can only be handled by stressing that they are not required to answer extremes only.

Likert Scale. Another method of countering the second objection to the Thurstone Scale is to offer a wider variety of answers. The Likert Scale normally offers a range of five choices:

Strongly agree
Agree more than disagree
Uncertain
Disagree more than agree
Strongly disagree.

An example of this type of scale would be:

1.	I always listen carefully to the instructions	SA	A	U	D	SD
2.	It is better to listen than to talk	SA	A	U	D	SD
3.	People always listen to what I say	SA	A	U	D	SD

The same arguments may be raised against this scale as with the Thurstone Scale, but again, any assessed ambiguity can be used as a group discussion item. As far as the second objection is concerned, there is a greater choice of answers. The choice may still not be sufficient, but there is doubt whether people can be more specific over a subjective element.

Self-assessment of attitudes. Apart from the specific knowledge determination test, most of the assessment approaches described so far require the learner to give an assessment of his own skills. This assessment must by necessity be subjective and can approach 100 per cent inaccuracy if the completer has little skill in self-assessment. The assessment is likely to be more objective if the questions relate to specific skills, rather than to attitudes and feelings.

One method of reducing the subjectivity is to administer the same questionnaire, not only to the learner but also to the learner's boss, and if possible to the learner's subordinates. It might be assumed that if these additional assessments are obtained, the final combined assessment must be complete.

This is not necessarily so, however, for a variety of reasons. The assessment by the boss may be very biased due to value judgements or simply because the boss sees the learner so rarely that his views are almost worthless. Subordinates are more likely to know the learner better, but they may have weak judgement or knowledge levels upon which to base their assessments.

In such an event, and particularly in cases where we are trying to assess attitudes or feelings rather than specific skills, the subjective views of the learners themselves may be the best we can hope for. Certain tests can, however, reduce the subjectivity.

A typical, initial self-assessment questionnaire, Figure 6.1, is one which I use in connection with the interpersonal skills training I offer. Any views expressed by individuals about themselves in this area must necessarily be highly subjective. The subsequent use of the same questionnaire will be discussed later when we consider immediate and longer-term outcome evaluation.

The format of this questionnaire is intended to provide a base level for each learner's skills or attitudes at the commencement of the training, or prior to the training, as the questionnaire is commonly completed prior to the learners attending the course. One has to assume that the questionnaire is completed honestly and with the maximum awareness of the individual into their own feelings. I have tried using parallel questionnaires with the learners' bosses and subordinates, but with unreliable results for the reasons cited earlier. The scale of ten is used in order to encourage the completer to assess the level as accurately as possible, or at least make them think hard about the rating, and it does not permit any assessment at an 'average' level. It has a further advantage, at a later stage, because it permits any movements to be expressed as a percentage increase or decrease.

Whatever the method used, and however subjective the approach may be, it is essential to obtain as extensive an initial assessment as possible about the learner's level. Without this assessment, further validation or evaluation has little meaning.

NAME _____   DATE _____

BEHAVIOUR SKILLS QUESTIONNAIRE

Please enter a tick in the space against each item on the scale 1 to 10 representing where you consider your present level of skill might be.

IN A GROUP AS A MEMBER OF THE GROUP

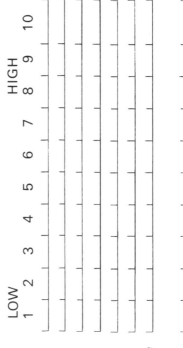

LOW   HIGH
1 2 3 4 5 6 7 8 9 10

1. Controlling amount of talking I do.
2. Being brief and concise.
3. Supporting others' ideas.
4. Building in others' ideas.
5. Being aware of my behaviour.
6. Initiating proposals and suggestions.
7. Explaining my disagreements with the points of view of others.
8. Controlling amount of giving own views.

84

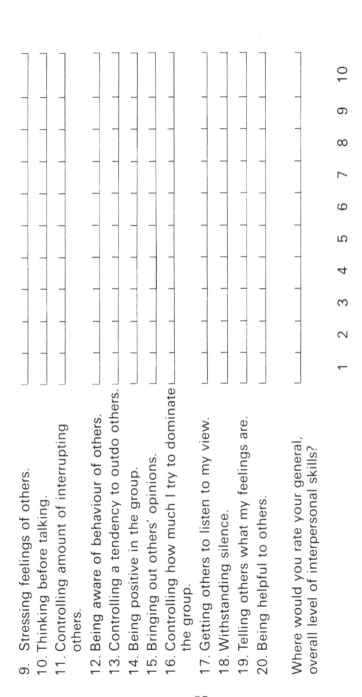

9. Stressing feelings of others.
10. Thinking before talking.
11. Controlling amount of interrupting others.
12. Being aware of behaviour of others.
13. Controlling a tendency to outdo others.
14. Being positive in the group.
15. Bringing out others' opinions.
16. Controlling how much I try to dominate the group.
17. Getting others to listen to my view.
18. Withstanding silence.
19. Telling others what my feelings are.
20. Being helpful to others.

Where would you rate your general, overall level of interpersonal skills?

1 2 3 4 5 6 7 8 9 10

Figure 6.1 Self-assessment questionnaire

7
ASSESSMENTS
DURING THE EVENT

Validation and evaluation are concerned with identifying the change which takes place from the state existing before the training event to that evolving after the training. But the trainer often needs to know *during* the training to what extent the training is having an effect. If the required changes are not taking place, it may be necessary to modify immediately the approach or the material. The acceptance of the need, to modify the training, and the ability to do so, reflects the flexibility of both the trainer and the training event and is itself a measure of validation.

Most of the direct tests of knowledge and skill described previously can be used at this interim stage, either as a repetition of the original test or an updated test related to what has occurred on the course so far. The tests may be administered formally or informally. If the formal approach is used, depending on what needs to be assessed, a written test of knowledge may be set or a practical activity tested. Assessment of the answers given in the knowledge test or the result of the practical test will give an objective indication of the progress of the learning.

The testing need not, of course, be formal or even obvious. Knowledge development can always be assessed by discreet questioning during a discussion. If all the learners have the opportunity to answer questions, their replies will reveal the extent of the learning.

Similarly, the specific test required can be included as part of a practical activity and its performance observed.

Observation must play an important part in assessment of learning during a training event, particularly in training other than for specific skills and knowledge.

ACTIVITY OBSERVATION

The exact nature of the observational method will depend on the type of activity involved and if observational aids are used, these too will vary with the activity.

At its simplest, observational assessment is practised by the trainer who has in mind a standard towards which the learners will be moving. The trainer's observation of the progress of the learners towards this standard will furnish an assessment of achievement. The observation of an experienced and skilled trainer who can compare a group or individual with other learners with whom he has worked should not be discounted. However, whatever the experience of the trainer and his attempts to make any assessment as objective as possible, there is always the danger that a considerable amount of subjectivity will remain. The level of subjectivity can be reduced if a quantitative or objective form of observation is used.

If the observation of an individual is open to accusations of subjectivity, these problems can be reduced by having more than one person make the observations and by using the multiple observations as the basis for assessment. This approach could of course be achieved by the use of a number of trainers, but is is rare for any training event to have such a luxury. Instead, if the training involves group training activities, the group itself can provide the multiple observations. However, unless we are dealing with a very experienced and advanced group, even multiple assessments may not compensate for reduced observational skills.

At its simplest the group performing the activity will also

act as its own observers and will be responsible for analysing the group's performance. This approach is fraught with many difficulties and although it is used extensively to train a group to be more aware of its own activities, it has less value as an assessment approach. If the group has been actively involved in a group task either the task or the observation can be simplified because of the dual requirements on the individuals. We can observe a parallel of this effect with the leader or chairman of a real life group who, if he becomes too involved in the task being performed by the group he is leading, finds that his control over the group will be reduced.

Some of the group can be withdrawn to act as observers and this approach can often increase the value of the observations. In what is commonly called the 'Fishbowl Approach', about six members are taken from a group of twelve to act as observers while the remaining six are required to perform a task. The advantage of this method is that the observers can concentrate on observing and the participants can concentrate on performing the task.

After the event, the activity can be assessed by a combination of the views of the participants, the observers and, if necessary, the trainer. Variations of the sequence are possible and it is sometimes desirable to use different approaches at different stages of a course. For example, the participants can be asked to comment on how they assess their own performance before allowing the observers to come in with their views. Finally the trainer can tie up any loose ends, perhaps arbitrate on any disagreements and comment on the favourable aspects of the activity since it is almost certain that the comments of the others will have concentrated on the less favourable aspects. Alternatively, the sequence with the participants and the observers can be reversed, giving the observers the first opportunity to comment. There is one almost invariable rule: the trainer must not be the first to comment. Depending on the trainer's power position, the trainer's views could contaminate those of the others, or the others could react against those views and thus introduce conflict.

The skill and experience of the observers will determine the value of the observational assessments. Even with observers who have little skill, improvements can be obtained by the use of observational guides or *aides-mémoire* which will at least concentrate the observers' attention on the areas requiring information. Many group observational guides are based on the Action Centred Learning approach of looking at the needs and actions relating to the task, the group and the individual. Figure 7.1 shows a typical aide-memoire for observers looking at a group decision-making activity.

This type of observational aide-memoire can be modified in many ways to suit the activity and its requirements. If the training is concentrating on the effective role of the chairman or leader of a meeting, the items for observation will relate to this role. For example

- how much did he bring members in?
- how effectively did he bring members in?
- how much did he involve the group in the decision-making?
- how much use of summaries did he make?

and so on.

Similar approaches can be used in the observation of one-to-one interactions or interviews. Figure 7.2 shows an aide-memoire which can be used to observe an interview practice, but, of course, other modifications can be made to suit other types of interaction.

In the same way that we found reporting back could vary when assessing the performance of groups, so can variations be applied to the assessment of an interview practice.

The approach commonly used after an interview practice is to ask the interviewer to comment firstly on his own performance. This quite often brings out most of the learning points which can be confirmed by the observer, who is the next to report. The observer may be able to reduce the self-criticism of some aspects of the interviewer and introduce some positive aspects. The interviewee can then be asked to comment from his viewpoint at the receiving end of the interview – a most important viewpoint in any interview.

OBSERVATION OF LEADER

Observe the leader closely during the activity and make short notes about any significant incidents related to the subject headings below.

Did the leader

TASK	Achieve the task? How successfully?
	Analyse and define the problem?
	Work to a plan?
	Test ideas, proposals and solutions?
	Make the best use of resources?
	Use all the information available or obtainable?
GROUP	Brief them effectively about the task?
	Reach agreement on the objectives?
	Agree the group process – timing, standards, decision procedures?
	Summarise progress? How often? How well?
	Encourage the group to work together?
	Control the group?
	Keep the group on the track?
	Involve all the members?
INDIVIDUAL	Give each member a job to do?
	Check the understanding of each individual about his job and the task?
	Investigate special skills and knowledge?
	Confirm the progress of each individual?
	Bring each person in as necessary?
	Ignore anybody?
	Visibly upset anybody?

Figure 7.1   Activity analysis

Structure

How did the interviewer start the interview?
Did the interviewer follow a structure?
Was this structure explained to the interviewee?
How did the interviewer terminate the interview?
Was the interviewer aware of the interviewee's
reaction to the interview?
If so, how was this achieved?

Behaviour

How quickly was rapport established?
Was the interviewee encouraged to talk?
How prescriptive was the interviewer?
Did the interviewer appear to listen?
Did the interviewer appear to be interested?

General

What were the three best aspects of the interview?
What were the three worst aspects of the interview?
How would you rate the interview as a whole?

Figure 7.2 Interview observation form

Finally, if anything remains to be said, the trainer can come
in. Perhaps the trainer's role will be to summarise and clarify
the comments and to add any omitted aspects which are
sufficiently important to warrant comment.

If there are a number of interview practices, the comments
of the observer, the interviewer and the interviewee can take
place in any combination of all three provided that the
trainer is always the last to come in, other than helping the
assessors make their comments.

AIDS TO OBSERVATION

In many cases the use of the participants themselves, with or without the addition of observers, is preferable to other forms of observation since they
- learn how to analyse an event by (painfully) working through one of their own
- gain practice in giving feedback to themselves and others
- learn how to use an analytical resource they always have available, themselves.

But it is sometimes necessary to consolidate the information available by observation and modern technology has given us two approaches we can use to support or replace the more traditional methods.

Audio equipment. The simplest equipment approach to observation is the use of the tape recorder. This equipment can record an event for later replay, when critical incidents can be identified, or the particular use of words or tones checked with the participant. While the event is being taped, the trainer or other observers will look out for incidents which need comment and will make a note of the position of the incident on the tape.

Audio recording is usually most effective in one-to-one training situations, not when recording a group event. The recording equipment and the microphone(s) must be unobtrusive and as a result the sound quality of a group recording may be poor, particularly at times of very high activity. The voice levels of different people may vary from distortion at one extreme and sound loss at the other, unless the microphones and equipment are highly sensitive and reactive, or there is an equipment operator available to monitor and maintain the balance.

Video equipment. Video equipment is more versatile than audio equipment as it incorporates both sound and vision facilities. Two approaches are possible – as a visual aid only or to provide a permanent recording.

One of the major problems encountered in observation, as active birdwatchers will be aware, is the physical presence of the observers. This presence can affect the performance of learners practising an interaction or task. If we remove this observational distraction, however, by removing the observers, we also remove the facility of giving observational feedback.

But if we remove the observers to another room and replace them with a TV camera linked with a receiver in the observation room, we have gone some way to resolving this problem. The observers can see and hear everything taking place but cannot themselves be seen or heard. In theory this is an ideal solution but, unfortunately, we have introduced another contaminatory factor – the camera. The participants are aware of the presence of the camera and there is the danger that they will over-act or over-react because of it. In practice, they do usually react at first, but eventually become less camera conscious and more natural as the event or the course progresses. Notice must be taken of this possibility and its effects taken into account in the appraisal. Afterwards, the observers and participants can come together in the traditional way to discuss what has happened.

A useful addition to the basic equipment which will help in the post event discussion is the video recorder. This can be used in the same way as the audio record, but it has wider possibilities and more impact as the participants are able to see themselves.

The ability to see oneself on a video recording has both advantages and disadvantages. Some people can become so obsessed with watching themselves that this gets in the way of seeing and hearing what they are doing. A disadvantage of video recording and audio recording is that feedback from its use can take much longer than when it is not used. And it *must* be used. There can be a very unfavourable reaction from trainees if television is used but the opportunity is not given to see the result.

As with audio recording, video recording is more effective with one-to-one or very small groups, for the same reasons – the constraints of sound and vision. Obviously a larger group can be recorded if there is perhaps a director, with three or more cameras to take in the whole group and different parts of the group. A compromise can be obtained using two fixed cameras and with the trainer operating a vision switcher, but the trainer can do little else while doing this.

The time problem can sometimes be reduced by letting the participants watch the recording in their own time or when they can be excused from an activity. From example, on a self-presentation course I have recorded an individual's presentation and used the recording minimally in an appraisal feedback immediately after the event. I have also used the whole recording, but when this happens the presenter does not take part in the next person's presentation. They sit elsewhere watching the video recording of their presentation (or as much of it as they can stand!). In this way the video recording is used, but little extra time is expended. A similar approach can be used for recordings on interview training courses, negotiation training, sales and marketing training and management of meetings courses.

Behaviour analysis. The use of general observational approaches, with or without observational aids, attempts to reduce the subjective nature of observation and assessment. Other approaches attempt to reduce subjectivity even further and behaviour analysis – described earlier – is one such successful tool. Its use can range from an analysis and feedback of a one-to-one interaction, through the observation, analysis and feedback of a chairman's skills, techniques and behaviours, to the observation of the process and progress of a whole group.

Feedback and discussion of the observations can vary according to the activities being observed. With most observational and feedback techniques it is common, and indeed expected, to discuss interview results immediately following the interaction. The process observation of a decision-making group, a negotiation activity or the skills of chairmanship also need to be considered immediately after an event. But when we are looking at, for example, the development of behavioural skills, it may be dangerous to look immediately at one isolated event.

Whenever I need to observe and analyse the behavioural skills of a group, I delay the publication of the results for as long as possible and certainly resist having to state them after the first activity. The behaviour of people varies considerably, for many reasons, from one event to another: an activity may not appeal to them; they may not know anything about the subject of an activity; the time of day may be having an effect on them, and so on. The publication of the behavioural observation after any activity may thus give a false picture overall, although accurate for that one isolated event. A more realistic behaviour pattern or profile is produced from a number of activities, although it is still necessary to look at the variations from one activity to another.

On interpersonal skills courses with which I am concerned I give the observational data feedback to the participants at the end of the third day, by which time they have performed some seven or more behavioural activities and are also ready to look at the data in terms of any necessary behaviour modification. Figure 7.3 shows a typical example of the profile feedback sheet for an individual on an interactive skills course. The horizontal rows represent the behavioural categories within which the individual has been observed. The vertical columns are used for each observed activity and record the number of contributions, the contributions identified with the relevant category and the raw number of contributions expressed as a percentage. The number of contributions are totalled for each activity and compared with the total contributions for the group expressed as a raw total and also a hypothetical average for the group. The contributions in each category are totalled, averaged and entered in the final vertical column to produce a general pattern or profile for each category.

Normally at this stage in an interactive skills course, the individuals make decisions based on this feedback on whatever behaviour modifications may be necessary. These plans when put into operation can be monitored by continued analysis and the eventual production of a 'Post-modification' profile.

Category / Activity	A	B	C	D	E	F	Average
PROPOSING	2 (2%)	6 (11%)			3 (16%)	1 (3%)	2 (5%)
SUGGESTING		1 (2%)					–
BUILDING		1 (2%)					–
SEEKING IDEAS		1 (2%)					–
SEEKING INFORMATION	14 (14%)	9 (17%)	3 (10%)	1 (3%)	4 (21%)	1 (3%)	5 (11%)
TESTING UNDERSTANDING	2 (2)	1 (2)					1 (2)
GIVING INFORMATION	43 (43)	23 (43)	19 (63%)	24 (77%)	7 (37)	16 (43)	22 (50)
DISAGREEING WITH REASONS	11 (11)					1 (3)	2 (5)
SUMMARISING							–
SUPPORTING	5 (5)	3 (6)	1 (3)	1 (3)	1 (5)		2 (5)
OPEN	1 (1)						–
DISAGREEING	1 (1)					1 (3)	–
ATTACKING						2 (5)	–
BLOCKING	9 (9)	2 (4)	7 (23)	1 (3)	3 (16)	7 (19)	4 (9)
BRINGING IN	1 (1)					2 (5)	1 (2)
SHUTTING OUT	12 (12)	6 (11)		4 (13)	1 (5)	6 (16)	5 (11)
n Individual / n Group (Group average)	$\frac{101}{396}$ (59)	$\frac{53}{250}$ (36)	$\frac{30}{390}$ (56)	$\frac{31}{249}$ (35)	$\frac{19}{145}$ (21)	$\frac{37}{289}$ (41)	44

Figure 7.3 Profile feedback sheet

Course audits. In addition to checking the progress of individuals, the progress of the course and the attitudes of the participants can be monitored with a view to modifying the material and approach if necessary.

This monitoring is often achieved by an audit at the end of the day's proceedings. The participants are asked such questions as

- what have you learned today?
- what helped the learning?
- was there anything which hindered your learning today?
- if so, how did this happen?
- was there anything you would have liked to have
    spent more time on?
    spent less time on?
    omitted?

The course participants are asked to complete an audit sheet containing these questions and are allowed about ten minutes at the end of each day for this purpose. The audit sheets are then given to the tutor who, before the following morning, summarises and analyses the information. The information is used initially as a discussion base at the start of the next day. This can often produce more than simply discussion for if the sheets show a common desire for more time to be spent on a particular topic (perhaps because the topic has not been accepted or understood completely) the tutor must take account of these statements. The normal progress of the course may be suspended so that some time can be taken to remedy the failure or omission; if this is not done the course will not progress effectively.

A simple but effective daily audit can be used without the need for a written statement at the end of each day's training. At the *start* of each training day, the course participants can be asked to each identify three words which reflect their feelings or views about the previous day and its training activities. The words from each participant are posted on a sheet of paper fixed to the training room wall. The words are offered to the group to be challenged or clarified and a lively period of discussion can ensue. Depending on the words and what arises from the discussion, the tutor can take any necessary action to extend the discussion or pursue aspects raised if the three-words audit identifies areas which require further action.

The results of this type of audit relate in many ways to the type of training. The approach is more relevant, but not completely so, to human relations training in some form – sales, negotiating, interviewing, interactions and so on. I have used this method at the start of each day on a team-building course and on one occasion the discussion resulting from the posting of the group's words lasted for the remainder of the morning, resulting in detailed feedback within the group. The method, however, is equally useful to the trainer involved in more mechanical training as it gives him continuous feedback on the attitude of the group to the training being offered and some measure of the understanding being achieved. For example, if the word 'confused' occurs several times in one morning, there are clear indications that the trainer has a problem to solve.

Session assessments. It is sometimes necessary for the trainer to be able to assess the progress of the training event in a more formal way than using the daily audit or the three-word approach. This can be done on either a session or a daily basis, and, although some benefits can be obtained from this 'immediate' feedback, one has to be aware of the possible dangers. The principal danger is that a session, for example, can be assessed in its own right; this is no problem so long as the session is self-contained within the course and does not depend on any other sessions or activities. This is not always the case, and it is more normal for a series of sessions and activities to be linked together and not stand alone. If the sessions are connected, there is the danger that if an assessment is made after each session, the views will be produced in isolation and can give a completely erroneous view. There is less danger where the assessment is made at the end of the day since the linked series will probably have been completed during this period. However, the same problems related to single sessions can occur if a series is only part completed at the end of the day. In such circumstances it will probably be more effective to leave the assessment to the end of the series, whenever this might occur.

The trainer must, of course, decide beforehand what immediate feedback is required and, more importantly, why it is needed. The 'why' is often ignored. There is little point in collecting information simply for the sake of collecting. If the assessments show something to be wrong the trainer is in danger of losing his credibility if he does nothing about it. He may not have the time to rectify any problems; if so then he should not be asking the questions.

Many immediate reaction assessments require the trainee simply to complete a tick list, whether the tick scales are based on Thurstone, Likert or semantic differential approaches. This will produce *some* information, but if the scale scores suggest that all is not well, there is no immediate indication of the nature of the problem. As fewer answers are required in this staged questionnaire than in a full end-of-course questionnaire, the questions can be more extensive. A typical format of this type of questionnaire is shown in Figure 7.4 below.

SESSION: THE MANAGEMENT CYCLE.

	1 2 3 4 5	
Interesting	└──┴──┴──┴──┘	Boring
Clear	└──┴──┴──┴──┘	Confusing
Simple	└──┴──┴──┴──┘	Complicated
Time too short	└──┴──┴──┴──┘	Time too long
Visual aids good	└──┴──┴──┴──┘	Visual aids poor
Should be retained	└──┴──┴──┴──┘	Should be omitted
Learned a lot	└──┴──┴──┴──┘	Learned little
Confirmed usefully a lot	└──┴──┴──┴──┘	Confirmed little

If your scoring for any element is 1, 2 or 3, please state why you have given this score.

If your scoring for any element is 4 or 5, please state why you have given this score.

If you have scored 1, 2 or 3 against the learning or confirmation elements, please state how you intend to implement this learning.

Figure 7.4   Session questionnaire

It will be seen from Figure 7.4 that there is the opportunity for learners to give feedback on current learning problems. If, for example, the assessment sheets are completed at the end of the day, the trainer must be prepared to summarise the information after the end of the training day and make plans to resolve the problems at the earliest opportunity.

Tutor assessments. The immediate reaction assessments described have all been concerned with the assessment of sessions, activities and the extent of learning. But a vital part of a training event is not only the material content but also the trainer involvement. The session assessment questionnaire described in Figure 7.4 will also give some indications of the learners' reactions to the trainer. For example, comments on whether they found the session interesting/boring, clear/confusng, simple/complicated, relate not only to the material but also the manner in which the trainer presented the material. On occasions a more in-depth study of the trainer's effectiveness is necessary. This will usually be needed by the trainer's boss, who will make observations, but often the people who can comment most realistically are those on the receiving end of the teaching – the learners.

Tutor assessment questionnaires must be introduced very carefully. I see many dangers when the trainer's boss introduces it and asks the learners to complete it. During a course a relationship develops between trainer and trainee, either good or bad, and this would probably be reflected in the extremes offered in a questionnaire set by the trainer's boss.

The same result could happen also if the questionnaire was set by the trainer, but the danger could be less if the trainer introduced it in a natural manner and was open with the group about the objectives for the assessment – namely so that the trainer can improve his skills. Whichever method is used, this assessment approach will always be sensitive to contamination, more so than session assessments as the learners are being asked to comment on a person rather than a thing. Figure 7.5 suggests part of a possible format for this kind of questionnaire.

Course: Session:

Tutor: Observer:

Date:

Introduction

		Very well	Well	Ade- quately	Badly/ Not at all
		1	2	3	4
1.	How well did he introduce the subject?	1	2	3	4
2.	How well did he describe the objectives?	1	2	3	4
3.	How well did he outline the content?	1	2	3	4
4.	How well did he outline the approach?	1	2	3	4

Main body of the session

5.	How well did he build the session up logically?	1	2	3	4
6.	How well were questions used?	1	2	3	4

and so on.

Figure 7.5   Tutor assessment questionnaire

OVER-USE OF TESTS

Trainers who use or see the need to use tests during training to obtain immediate reaction assessments must be aware of a very real danger: the adverse reaction of the learners to the tests or assessments. If they have to complete frequent questionnaires this completion can become boring and tedious and it can become counter-productive to continue the practice. The learners may be too weary to perform yet another task at the end of the training day and may be anxious to get away to dinner, the bar or bed. Consequently, completion may be either superficial or 'chance' answers only may be given. If assessments of a detailed nature are delayed until the following morning, there may have been some memory loss, something which may be significant in itself particularly if a pattern develops.

So the trainer cannot anticipate 100 per cent success or co-operation, but must try to strike a balance somewhere between minimum and maximum use of tests if he is to be aware at all of how the training event is progressing and how much learning is being achieved.

8
END OF EVENT VALIDATION

The second important validation event occurs at the end of the training programme, the first being any assessments or tests prior to or at the start of the training. The testing during the event is also important but, bearing in mind the dangers of over-testing, the validation scheme would still be successful if the interim stage was omitted.

It is at this end-of-training validation stage that we can differentiate between internal and external validation. Internal validation can be considered to be the assessment of the validity of the training course itself. Were the training techniques the most appropriate? Was the content appropriate for the training group? Was the training conducive to learning? Internal validation therefore relates to the training; external validation, on the other hand, relates to the extent to which the learners have learned from the training experience.

In previous chapters a variety of validation measures have been described, some of which can be used not only at the pre-training stage and during the interim stages, but also at the end of training stage, in both internal and external validation. The similarity of uses is logical since in validation we are trying to assess changes between a pre- and post-training situation, along a continuum of training. It is obviously essential that the two extreme tests can be compared directly, otherwise validation has no reality. There is no necessity for the two tests to be identical, only comparable, as the change produced may be the addition of new skills rather than the remedying of deficient skills.

Most of the validation approaches and instruments have already been described, so their post-training role will be discussed only briefly here, although there are some approaches which one would normally find as end-of-course approaches.

INTERNAL VALIDATION APPROACHES

Let us firstly consider validation approaches concerned with the training event itself.

Group review. The most common method of validating a training course, and one which has been most widely used since training was introduced, is the group review. At the end of the course, usually as the last event, the group of learners is brought together in order to hear them state verbally their views about various aspects of the training. Unfortunately, even though good relationships may have been constructed between the learners and the tutors, it is most unlikely that the comments will be completely forthright and comprehensive.

An approach which is more likely to produce realistic results is when the full course group is divided into smaller groups and each small group is asked to review the course. People are more likely to say what they have on their minds when in a small group rather than in full session, and the other members of the group might convince them that they are being either too hard or too soft. Some leads might be given to the groups by the tutors about the aspects which they should concentrate upon or cover, but care must be taken not to contaminate the views with an excess of direction.

Once the small groups have identified the main comments they wish to make, the groups are brought together for a full group review. Spokespeople will have been appointed in each group so the comments can be completely open and anonymous.

The principal advantage of this method is that validation feedback from the group is immediate and can be questioned for clarification, provided the tutor does not give the impression of being defensive with this questioning.

There are, however, a number of disadvantages to the approach. As the event is at the end of the training course, the members may be legitimately anxious to get away and, as a result, may not put much effort into the activity. So timing is important and, if validation is accorded the importance that it should receive, sufficient programmed time should be left for this purpose.

There is also the danger that a vocal minority might exert an undue influence over the majority and full views may not be expressed. Division into small groups may reduce this danger but the vocal objectors may still exert undue influence when the groups come together again.

End-of-course questionnaires. The trainer will wish to know how much the learners have enjoyed the training course, how much they have learned from it, what they thought of the sessions in terms of clarity and interest, and so on. Feedback of this nature can be obtained from questionnaires completed by the course participants at the end of the course. Such questionnaires have been discussed when we were looking at immediate reaction levels during the course, and information was obtained at the end of sessions or at the end of the training day. End-of-course information can be obtained by extending this approach. Various methods are available and some will depend on whether immediate reaction questionnaires have been used during the progress of the course.

If immediate reaction questionnaires have not been used, one method might be to give the learners a questionnaire covering the complete course. If it has been a long course, this method can produce a very long questionnaire, particularly if the simple tick lists are extended by in-depth questions as suggested earlier. Even without these extensions, much is being demanded of the learners and the answers given may therefore not be realistic. The advantage of this approach is that the learners can look back over the course and assess the content, weighing up the relationship of one part with another. However, there is the danger that the earlier parts of the course may receive scant treatment as so much will have happened subsequently.

If, of course, assessment has continued during the course with end-of-session, end-of-day or end-of-section questionnaires being completed at these intervals, the burden of completion becomes much less. All that may remain to be completed is the final section of the course and any final comments. It is strongly recommended that if this approach is to be used, the cumulative completion of an in-depth questionnaire is certainly the most useful, as anything less can degenerate into a tick-list.

Tick-lists which have numbers allocated to high, medium and low scorings can be dangerous if this approach is looked upon as a highly mathematic and scientific method. It is, of course, far from being so, although many trainers perform mathematical calculations and treat the answers as absolute instead of the indications which they really are. It is even worse when the totals and averages produced are used to compare disparate aspects. Totals and averages of the scorings are useful, but it must always be remembered that they are only indications.

Another danger which can emerge is related to the words which are used in the semantic differential scale method. There is considerable difference between a scale which asks learners to classify their views of a course as 'Excellent to Bad' and 'Good to not too good.'

It is less likely that markings would be given at the extreme ends of the scale in the first case than in the second case, but what value would be obtained from the extremes in the second scale? Although an 'extreme' scoring might be given, there will still be a considerable latitude in the range which would go unrecorded. Even worse, in a group of people whose organisational climate virtually forbids them ever to score appraisals in the extremes there would be great problems. In the Excellent/Bad example, a top rating might be one down from Excellent, equalling 'Very Good indeed'.

However, because of the tendency to avoid extremes, if the Good/Not too good scale was used, a ranking just below the Good would be read as 'Adequate' – quite different from 'Very Good Indeed'.

Some validators are so suspicious of rating scales and their relationship with 'happiness sheets' that they will not use them at all. Instead they feel that a freedom of approach on the part of the learners will produce superior results. This freedom is achieved by asking the learners to comment on the course, its value and their learning, the comments not being in response to any direct questions. The learners are given a blank sheet of paper and the aspects on which they report, to what level and to what extent being left to them.

The theory behind this approach is that what the learners write down must be important aspects as far as they are concerned since they have been motivated to comment on those aspects. The theory, although excellent, may be faced with barriers, some of which have already been mentioned. If time is short, comments may be scanty and not represent what the learners really think as this will require a lot of consideration. The absence of any lead at all may result in comments not being made about earlier stages of the course, although this absence may indeed indicate that the earlier stages made no impact on the learner. The biggest problem, however, is for the validator who has little opportunity to collate and correlate the comments. This may not be necessary if the concern is purely with the learning of an individual, but if the learning has to be related to that of the group, then these difficulties are real.

There is a half-way stage between the scoring sheet and the blank sheet. In this approach, open textual comments are invited but in answer to some broad questions, such as

- What have you learned from the course? How? Why those aspects?
- Should any parts of the course be omitted?
- Should anything be included in the course which does not already appear?
- Any other comments?

A further possible compromise is to combine a limited numeric scale with some textual comments. The scale questions will be those which need to be collated in an arithmetical or quasi-arithmetical way, and are such that they lend themselves to this approach. An example of this mixed approach is shown in Figure 8.1.

If sufficient time is given for the trainees to formulate and record their thoughts, a considerable amount of feedback can be obtained over a wide range of topics. This wide range may mean that comparison between the reports and collation of the comments may be more difficult than with the tick lists, but perhaps a more realistic appraisal is being made.

Feelings review. The compromise between the blank sheet approach and the structured questionnaire is particularly valuable when we are considering validation of very general forms of training such as we find in the human relations area. The structured approach is very satisfactory when attempting to validate training which is highly structured, such as a series of specific knowledge inputs or discrete skill activities. However, when the training is unstructured or is very learner-centred, this structured approach runs into difficulties of definition in what is to be validated. The structured, specific approach is the nearest one can get to a quantitative, objective assessment of objective training methods, an impression being heightened by the apparently mathematical nature of the instrument. But, if the training is itself of a subjective nature, then the best we can hope for is a subjective assessment – in fact, for subjective training the most appropriate method of approach may be the subjective approach. Facts are objective, feelings are subjective, so an assessment of feelings will necessarily also be a subjective one.

The feelings review approach is commonly used in human relations training where feelings rather than facts abound. This is particularly so in interpersonal or interactive skills training. The questionnaire following the sense of the training elicits the real feelings and attitudes of the participants in the terms used during the training itself. In

NAME_____

INTERPERSONAL SKILLS TRAINING

In order to maintain our learning events at the level required by you, our clients, we need to know to what extent the course has met your needs. Would you please complete the following as openly as possible.

Course objectives met	└─┴─┴─┴─┴─┴─┘	Not met
My objectives met	└─┴─┴─┴─┴─┴─┘	Not met
Course too long	└─┴─┴─┴─┴─┴─┘	Too short
Tutor helpful	└─┴─┴─┴─┴─┴─┘	Unhelpful
Tutor too directive	└─┴─┴─┴─┴─┴─┘	Too non-directive
Course as a whole good	└─┴─┴─┴─┴─┴─┘	Poor
Would recommend	└─┴─┴─┴─┴─┴─┘	Wouldn't

Which parts of the course did you find most helpful?

Which parts of the course did you find least helpful?

Are there any parts of the course you would omit?

Is there anything else you would have liked to have seen in the course?

Any other comments?

Figure 8.1   End-of-course questionnaire

this approach, free and far-ranging comments are obtained. However, the format does not allow an easy comparison between the answers of individuals as is possible with a numeric scale. Perhaps there is much to be said for this 'disadvantage' in that the validation answers have to be read more closely than a set of simple numbers.

One example of this approach is shown in Figure 8.2 which shows a feelings questionnaire used at the end of an interpersonal skills course. This questionnaire demonstrates the range and variety of questions which can be asked if the training has led to this level of openness between the participants and the tutor.

Action planning. Although not specifically a validation approach, action planning can be complementary to any form of validation or evaluation. One of the problems associated with training courses is ensuring that any learning is transferred to the learner's real world of work. The learner may leave the training course having learned and with every intention of putting the learning into practice. But when the learner arrives back at work, pressure of work, lack of interest by boss and colleagues, active disagreement with the new ideas and practices on the part of the boss and colleagues and so on, may demotivate the learner who will slip back to pre-training ways.

If before leaving the course, however, the learner has produced a plan of action containing a realistic number of items to be introduced back at work and he contracts with himself to introduce them, there is a greater likelihood that something will happen. The chances of success will improve if a small number of aims only are selected, aims which the learner sees as having a reasonable chance of success. Subsequent action plans can be made when the initial items have been achieved.

A copy of the action plan can be left with the trainer or validator who can contract to get in touch with the learner at a later stage to determine the success or otherwise of the plan. At the very least the learner knows that there is somebody who is interested in the plan and its progress. Trainers who have made this arrangement with the learner

Name _____   Date _____

INTERPERSONAL SKILLS REVIEW

1. The major feeling I have about this learning event is . . . . . .

2. If this course had been a film, a play or a book, the title would have been . . . . . .

3. The part(s) of the event I enjoyed most . . . . . .

4. The part(s) of the experience I can make most use of . . . . . .

5. Something I learned, or had usefully confirmed about myself is . . . . . .

6. Something I learned, or had usefully confirmed about other people is . . . . . .

7. The part(s) of the event I enjoyed least was(were) . . . . . .

8. The part(s) of the event I can make least use of is(are) . . . . . .

9. If I were starting this experience again I would . . . . . .

10. One thing I regret having done is . . . . . .

11. One thing I regret not having done is . . . . . .

12. Right now I am feeling . . . . . .

Figure 8.2   Feelings review questionnaire

often receive feedback that their subsequent interest has acted as a spur to the learner to complete putting the action plan into practice.

The ideal way of attempting to ensure that the action plan has a chance of succeeding is, of course, to take positive steps to include the boss. With the learner's agreement, a copy of the action plan can be sent to the boss together with an invitation to discuss it with the learner. This action would only be necessary when prior arrangements to do this have not been made or when it is known that it would not happen as a matter of course. An alternative approach is for the learner to take positive action to involve the boss by deliberately seeking the boss's interest and involvement in the action plan.

Interview approach. A time-consuming, but valuable, assessment of the training is obtained by interviewing the course participants. Extended individual views of a person can be obtained in this way with the trainer clarifying any doubts or uncertainties during the interview. An interview is most valuable as it frequently happens that when an end-of-course validation sheet has been completed for the trainer and the learner has gone, it is discovered that an ambiguous statement or unclear remark or rating has been given. Unfortunately, the interviewing of each course participant, however desirable though it might be, is too time-consuming in most cases to make it a realistic approach.

Immediate or delayed validation. There are a number of reasons why doubts may be raised as to whether any means of validation should be attempted immediately at the end of the training event or whether there should be any delay. At the end of a course time may be too restricted to allow an effective validation to take place. When time is restrictive it may be best to delay any action, as realistic comments are unlikely if the learner has one eye on the finishing clock. If, however, any validation, particularly the completion of an assessment questionnaire is delayed, the learner has time to assess his reactions to the training away from what is often the euphoria at the end of a course. Later it may be possible to assess the learning in the cold light of the real working environment.

A delayed response has problems when the real world exerts its influence on the training world. If end-of-course questionnaires, for example, are not completed at the end of the training course, there is always the danger that they will not be completed at all. Immediate pressures of work or other important distractions may delay the completion and return of the questionnaire, and the longer the delay the greater the likelihood that the questionnaire will not be returned. I have seen no definitive research on return rates in such circumstances, but personal experience and reports by others seems to indicate a return rate of between thirty and sixty per cent.

EXTERNAL VALIDATION APPROACHES

Perhaps even more important than internal validation is external validation, or validation of the learning achieved by the course participants. It is of very little use if the training approach, content and methods are validated as effective if the learners cannot put the learning into practice. We are attempting to assess the element of change which we have agreed is the reason for training.

Validation of knowledge increase. In the validation of any knowledge increase, tests of a formal nature must play a significant part. The use of knowledge tests enabled us to assess the initial standards of the learners and, if it was found desirable, further tests indicated progress as the course proceeded. It should be a simple validation test to re-apply the initial test and determine the difference between the two scores. This is simple in practice, but a number of factors can interfere with making it an absolute test of knowledge increase.

In common with any other form of examination of a formal, written nature, the test shows that an individual knows or does not know the answers to the questions set *on the day and at the time in question*. With such a test we have no way of knowing whether the individual *understands* the information rather than simply knowing the answer. It might be that all that is required is knowledge of the right answer without knowing the reason why, but since we are considering training for practical application at work, academic knowledge alone rarely has a place.

Although it may reduce the opportunity for simple and direct comparison with an earlier test, a more realistic test may be a major activity which the learners must perform accurately. The activity will include the need to have the knowledge which would otherwise be tested in a direct examination. But here the information is an integral part of the activity and the learners may not even know they are being tested.

If, however, tests have to be applied, they can take any of the forms described earlier in Chapter 6, page 70 onwards:

- open answer
- binary choice
- multiple choice
- short answer.

It is not simple to produce any of these questionnaires and tests and if they are to have any real use in assessing training validity, they must be both reliable and valid. This means that such variables as the choice of words and so on must be considered and checked.

Validation of skills. The validation of skills is no easier at the end of the course than it is at the beginning or during the middle, and basically involves a repetition of the previous assessments.

Practical application. It is generally accepted that if a change has occurred during the training course, provided this change is in step with the objectives, the training is validated. The confirmation of the attainment of a new skill is much more difficult than confirming the acquisition of new knowledge. There is very little value in setting a written test to assess the possession of skills. If we set a problem relating to the skill in the form of a written question, a variety of responses are possible. Let us take, for example, an interviewing course concentrating on counselling techniques. At the end of the course a number of questions can be asked:

- what would you do if . . .
- given the opportunity, what planning would you do?
- how many stages would you go through during the interview?

The learner has a number of options in answering these questions

- he can answer them honestly and to the best of his ability
- he can answer them in the way he assumes the trainer would wish him to answer
- he can answer them in the way he believes the text book answers would be given
- he can answer in any way – rationally or irrationally.

Only the first option will give a very satisfactory confirmation of learning.

Although it leaves much to be desired, an approach with a greater likelihood of success in validation is to parallel the knowledge assessment activity described earlier. This may involve the use of role plays and case studies and consequently produce an assessment under artificial conditions, but it does permit the direct observation of skill. If the course has concentrated on one aspect of skill, one case study can be mounted to test the skills of the learner to the maximum amount possible. If, however, a number of aspects are covered during the course, unless these can be integrated in the one study, it will be necessary to have a series of assessments at the end of each stage.

While the practice interview or other activity is taking place it can be observed and appraised in one of the ways described earlier. If the level of skill had been determined at an early stage of the course, any change in skill would become apparent. Obviously much of this appraisal will be of a subjective nature if the skills in question are not of a technical or practical nature.

Assessment is much more straightforward if the skills involved are of a technical or practical nature. If this is so a specific practical test can be set, the results of which are then assessed against the skill level determined by the training need.

Behaviour analysis. Assessment of change is even more difficult when the training is concerned with attitude and behavioural skills changes. Most observations in these cases will be subjective. However, where there is the need to observe behaviours with a view to effecting a change or modification in them, a more objective instrument of observation can be used. We have seen earlier that behaviour analysis can be used throughout a course to plot the development of a behaviour pattern. It has also been shown how this pattern can be brought to the attention of the learners in a matrix form, with the suggestion that the data can be used to plan any behaviour modification necessary. Behaviour analysis can be continued and any modification recorded as some validation of change. The statement is qualified by use of the word 'some' since, although the behavioural observation may be accurate, the observation may not necessarily represent any real learning. The individual or group may behave in the way which is appropriate to the behavioural model which will be the basis of the training, but performance at the appropriate level on the course need not necessarily mean that this performance will be transferred to work – the learners may simply be pandering to the trainer. However, it is all we are in a position to observe and we have to be satisfied with it as being all that is possible to judge at this stage.

Repertory Grid. It was suggested earlier that attitudes, feelings and the attributes of various jobs can be determined prior to or at the beginning of training by an interview utilising the repertory grid approach. As with many of the other approaches suggested, the repertory grid can be repeated at the end of the event. The differences can then be compared with the earlier completion and analysed. The repertory grid approach has an advantage over some other interview methods in that the interviewer has much less direct involvement and hence there is less likelihood of interviewer contamination.

Semantic Differential Questionnaire. When we are attempting to validate learning which is almost wholly concerned with behavioural and attitudinal skills there are many difficulties in the way of producing an objective test. In fact, as we are dealing with almost completely subjective aspects it may be too much to seek an objective assessment.

If self-diagnosed attitudes have been obtained at the start of a course by means of diagnostic questionnaires constructed with Thurstone or Likert scales, the questionnaire can be repeated at the end of the course. Any differences between the two can be discussed and assessed as evidence of change, usually, however, in conjunction with other assessment aids.

It must be recognised that we are dealing not only with highly subjective results, but also with questionnaires which are highly susceptible to false answers, whether deliberate or not.

These questionnaires are more difficult to compare than the one based on semantic differentials to which a numerical weighting can be added easily. Again one has to be careful and not assume that this makes the approach really quantitative and objective. This is not so: all it does is to make comparisons easy and thus help identify significant changes.

The form of the semantic differential questionnaire used at the end of the training is exactly the same as the one used at the beginning of or before the training. Both forms are then compared and analysed for indications of change. This is the classic Pre- and Post-Test approach. However, when we are looking at behavioural and attitudinal changes there are serious shortcomings to this simple approach.

If we are assessing a course on supervisory or management skills, one of the aspects we would want to look at would be the learner's use of time. Consequently, at the start of the training we could ask a question related to the learner's management of time and ask for a self-rating on a scale of ten. A typical approach could be:

Use of time at work

Badly controlled   1 2 3 4 5 6 7 8 9 10   Well controlled

At the start of the course an individual might rate himself at scale 7, that is to say assessing himself is as quite skilled, though not exceptionally skilled, in the use of time. As the assessment is self-generated the rating must necessarily be subjective, but at least if we use the questionnaire on more than one occasion, the subjective judgements are all made from the same base.

If the same questionnaire is used as an end-of-course validation test, the traditional Pre- and Post-Test approach has been fulfilled. As the questionnaires are identical we can compare the results on an apparently reasonable basis. At the start of the course the time use element was rated at 7; let us assume that at the end of the course it is rated at 8. Taking into account that the comparison is not accurately arithmetical, there is an increase of identified skill of some 10 per cent. This is not an exceptional increase in skill, but remember that the initial assessment was 7 – not a bad level of skill to start with.

However, there are several other possibilities which might be usefully considered. The assessment of 7 may have been an accurate one and therefore the increase of 10 per cent skill may be realistic. But there may have been some aspects of self-delusion in the initial rating, and, though the end rating may be more realistic than the initial rating, the increase in skill of 10 per cent may not reflect the true increase.

This result will almost certainly be the result of contamination of the individual's assessment by the training: the learner will almost certainly have had his awareness and perceptions heightened as a result of the training.

THE 3-TEST APPROACH

One way of attempting to test the results of this possible contamination is to introduce a third completion of the same questionnaire. After the questionnaire has been completed for the second time, at the end of the course, the learner is asked to complete it again, a third time. But on this occasion he is asked to complete it as if he were completing it at the beginning of the course *but with his current perception of his skill* – in other words, knowing what he knows now. Let us assume in this example that the score of 7 was at a higher level than it was in reality. Consequently when the learner completed the questionnaire for the third time with new awareness, a true initial level gave a score of 3. This showed that the increase in skill from 3 to 8 was of the order of 50 per cent rather than 10 per cent. When this increase was compared with other observations of skill practice and the learner's own views of skill increase, an increase of about 50 per cent seemed to be a more realistic validation of the training.

I have used this 3-Test approach on a number of different training courses, particularly those concerned with human relations training. At the start of an interpersonal skills training course the learners complete the self-assessment questionnaire shown in Figure 8.3. This completion is designated completion 1. The same questionnaire is used again at the end of the course and on this occasion is designated completion 2. Finally, in order to obtain the more realistic assessment without training contamination, the questionnaire is administered again as completion 3.

From these three questionnaires comparisons can be made through use of the rating scores, but the warning must be repeated that although we are dealing with numerical ratings, the base data is still highly subjective. The comparisons can be made to show differences not only between completion 2 (the end of training completion) and completion 1 (the original initial completion) but also between completion 2 and completion 3 (the re-assessed starting level).

Figure 8.4 shows a summary of the completed questionnaires with the comparisons added. The figures show that when the end of course assessments (column 2) are compared with the initial assessments (column 1) there has been an increase in skill in some elements, no change in others and a slight decrease in skill in others, within a range – 10 per cent to + 30 per cent. When the individual changes are totalled the result is an overall increase in skill of 19 per

NAME

DATE

BEHAVIOUR SKILLS QUESTIONNAIRE

1 2 3 4

Please enter a tick in the space against each item on the scale 1 to 10 representing where you consider your present level of skill might be.

IN A GROUP AS A MEMBER OF THE GROUP

	LOW								HIGH	
	1	2	3	4	5	6	7	8	9	10

1. Controlling amount of talking I do.
2. Being brief and concise.
3. Supporting others' ideas.
4. Incorporating others' ideas.
5. Being aware of my behaviour.
6. Initiating proposals and suggestions.
7. Explaining my disagreements with the points of view of others.
8. Controlling amount of giving own views.

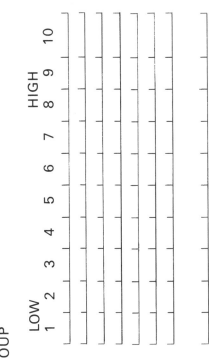

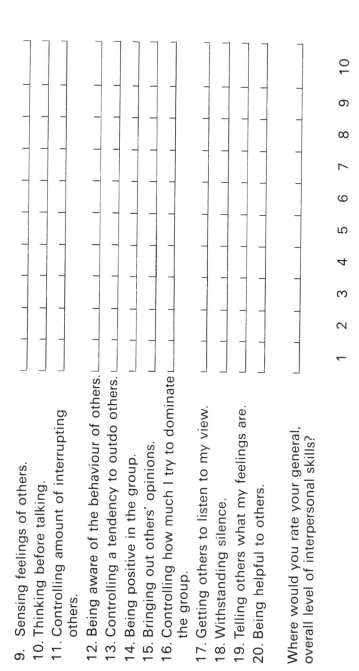

9. Sensing feelings of others.
10. Thinking before talking.
11. Controlling amount of interrupting others.
12. Being aware of the behaviour of others.
13. Controlling a tendency to outdo others.
14. Being positive in the group.
15. Bringing out others' opinions.
16. Controlling how much I try to dominate the group.
17. Getting others to listen to my view.
18. Withstanding silence.
19. Telling others what my feelings are.
20. Being helpful to others.

Where would you rate your general, overall level of interpersonal skills?

1   2   3   4   5   6   7   8   9   10

Figure 8.3   3-Test approach: Self-assessment questionnaire

Category	COLUMN 1 (Initial)	COLUMN 2 (Terminal)	COLUMN 3 (Revised initial)
In a group as member of the group			
1. Controlling amount of talking	4	7 (+3)	4 (+3)
2. Being brief and concise	4	4 (–)	4 (–)
3. Supporting others' ideas	5	5 (–)	5 (–)
4. Building on others' ideas	5	6 (+1)	3 (+3)
5. Being aware of my behaviour	5	7 (+2)	4 (+3)
6. Initiating proposals and suggestions	7	6 (–1)	5 (+1)
7. Explaining my disagreement with the points of view of others	7	6 (–1)	5 (+1)
8. Controlling amount of giving own views	5	5 (–)	3 (+2)
9. Sensing feelings of others	4	7 (+3)	3 (+4)
10. Thinking before talking	4	7 (+3)	3 (+4)
11. Controlling amount of interrupting others	5	6 (+1)	3 (+3)
12. Being aware of behaviour of others	6	8 (+2)	2 (+6)
13. Controlling tendency to outdo others	7	7 (–)	7 (–)
14. Being positive	6	7 (+1)	8 (–1)
15. Bringing out others' opinions	7	7 (–)	4 (+3)
16. Controlling how much I try to dominate the group	6	4 (–2)	3 (+1)
17. Getting others to listen to my views	7	8 (+1)	8 (–)
18. Withstanding silence	4	7 (+3)	3 (+4)
19. Telling others what my feelings are	4	7 (+3)	2 (+5)
20. Being helpful to others	8	8 (–)	7 (+1)
General overall level of interpersonal skills	6	6 (–)	4 (+2)
		(Total 19)	(Total 45)

Figure 8.4 Summary of questionnaire answers

cent. However, as we are considering a course which is concerned with increasing awareness, it is safe to assume that the initial assessment was incorrectly made by learners who have awareness problems. The end of course results can therefore be more realistically compared with a reassessed starting position, since by the end of the course it is again safe to assume that awareness has increased. Consequently when we compare column 2 with the reassessed views of completion 3, certain changes are observable. There are still some decreases in skill, but these are smaller and fewer in number: some decreases have become increases, some of the 'no changes' have now become increases and many of the increases have become bigger increases. The sum of the changes has now become a total increase of 45 per cent compared with the Pre/Post test of 19 per cent.

However, one has to be very careful in an interpretation of comparative assessments such as those under discussion, since a successful validation can produce widely different results from those described above.

Figure 8.5 shows increases of the order of 45 per cent between the end-of course assessment (column 2) and the initial assessment (column 1). But column 3 shows instead that the learner assesses the increase from the initial *real* state as much less than 45 per cent: rather the realistic increase appears as 21 per cent. Some situations can be worse than this with the column 3 result showing a minus score where the column 2 figure has a positive increase rating. Such results can suggest to the trainer that the learning event, for that individual at least, has been a failure or a partial failure.

This was certainly my reaction when this first happened to me, but I was fortunately able to discuss the results with the learner after the course. What emerged was that the learner had realised that he had been unrealistic in his relatively low assessments of his initial skills. This realisation came when he was required to complete the reassessed questionnaire. Negative results also appear when the end-of-course results are low. Learners have explained that far from being a failure, the course has been a complete success and awareness has increased many times. This awareness, however, and the resulting behaviour changes necessary

Category	Column 1	Column 2	Column 3
1	4	7 (+3)	7 (+3)
2	4	7 (+3)	7 (+3)
3	4	7 (+3)	6 (+2)
4	3	6 (+3)	4 (+1)
5	3	7 (+4)	5 (+2)
6	3	6 (+3)	5 (+2)
7	3	4 (+1)	5 (+2)
8	3	8 (+5)	3 (−)
9	3	7 (+4)	6 (+3)
10	3	5 (+2)	5 (+2)
11	3	6 (+3)	3 (−)
12	4	6 (+2)	5 (+1)
13	5	4 (−1)	3 (−2)
14	6	4 (−2)	3 (−3)
15	4	5 (+1)	5 (+1)
16	3	4 (+1)	6 (+3)
17	3	5 (+2)	3 (−)
18	3	7 (+4)	3 (−)
19	4	5 (+1)	4 (−)
20	6	7 (+1)	6 (−)
Overall	3	5 (+2)	4 (+1)
		TOTAL 45	TOTAL 21

Figure 8.5 Statistical comparison of questionnaire answers

were so radical that the learner has needed much more time than was available on the course to come to terms with them.

My experience has been that the 3-Test approach produces much more realistic results (not necessarily 'better') than the Pre/Post test approach, although it must be recognised that the method is still sensitive to subjective treatment. This subjectivity, of course, is found in any form of self-assessment.

9
AFTER THE EUPHORIA

It is often said that assessments or validations of training made at the end of a training event can suffer from a serious contamination which will cast serious doubts on any results. If the course has been a highly successful and enjoyable experience, the learners can be so pleased with themselves and the event that they are in a state of euphoria. In this emotive state, particularly as they are saying 'goodbye' to their fellow students with whom they may have formed particular relationships, views expressed on the training may be clouded. It is quite possible that on a scale of 1 to 10 the ratings given may be 3 or 4 ratings more than should realistically be given. It is because of these emotions that end-of-course questionnaires have been christened, often unfairly, 'happiness sheets'.

Apart from any other considerations, delaying any assessment beyond the immediate end of the course serves the purpose of allowing the clouding emotions to subside to a more rational level. But evaluation and validation attempts at a later stage than at the end of the course have distinct reasons and it is then that evaluation becomes more important than validation.

DELAYED EVALUATION APPROACHES

Evaluation can usefully be attempted some three to six months after the training event, while it is still reasonably fresh in the minds of the learners. It is also sufficiently distant from the training to have allowed the learners to start practising the skills learned.

Many of the approaches already discussed can be employed at this stage, but probably the biggest change is that the learner's work can be included in the evaluation. Other people can also be involved – the learner's boss, peers and subordinates. One thing, however, that has to be kept in mind is that the others may or may not be capable of assessing the worth of the person being evaluated. For example, a learner who has attended an interpersonal skills programme may be now more skilled in interpersonal interactions than his boss. In fact it may have been the boss who should have attended the course before the subordinate! In such a case, any assessment by the boss would be highly suspect. The boss and the others used in the assessment must also have a reasonable amount of contact with the learner so that they have sufficient evidence on which to base an assessment.

Inclusion of others. At what can be described as the intermediate evaluation stage, the obvious approach is to the learners themselves. The danger in doing this is that any assessment of learning or success in putting the learning into practice must be a subjective assessment of the individual. This may not be unrealistic in the circumstances, although, unless the individual is very aware of his own skills, the assessment might be very biased.

The next logical approach could be made to the learner's boss. However, as suggested earlier, one must be certain that the boss

- sees enough of the learner's work to be able to make a realistic judgement of a change from previous practice to the new improved state
- is able to make an objective judgement of the learner

without bias of some subjective value judgements, such as liking or disliking the learner
- is sufficiently skilled to assess the learner's skill level.

Similar requirements exist if we wish to involve the learner's peers although they are often more likely to satisfy the contact criterion than the boss.

If the learner has subordinates to manage or supervise, in some respects these are the best assessors to approach as the activities of the learner impinge directly on them. They should almost certainly satisfy the contact criteria, but may fall well short as far as other criteria are concerned.

A combination of assessments will have more substance or objectivity than one alone, although there is no guarantee that a number of insubstantial assessments will produce a well-based and objective evaluation. Possible combinations could usefully include the following

- learner and peers
- learner and subordinates
- learner and boss
- learner, subordinates and boss
- learner, peers and boss
- learner, peers, subordinates and boss.

Control groups. The value of involving a control group which has not been subjected to the training has been described earlier. This requirement is an absolute necessity when we are trying to evaluate learning over a period of time, as so many factors can contaminate the apparent learning. Both the control group and the trained group can change over the period, with many of the changes not being attributable to the training, even in the case of the training group. Such non-attributable factors can include the issue of improved guidance or instructions for the job, a natural progression of development as a result of exposure to the work, enforced development due to pressures of various kinds, and so on. Many of these factors could fall equally on the trained and control groups. Consequently, although the absence of a control group could materially affect the objectivity of an evaluation, the presence does not necessarily guarantee complete objectivity.

Action planning. A very positive ending to a training event has been seen to be the production of an action plan by the learner, a plan which the learner was committed to implement. Such action plans can be used in a number of ways, especially as assessments of the extent to which the learner has implemented the learning. The extent of implementation can suggest how much the individual really learned from the experience.

Three or four months after the end of the learning event an assessment can be made of the learning extent by asking the learner to refer to the plan and analyse the practical results. Preferably this analysis should be the result of an agreement between the learner and the boss, but, in the absence of such an agreement, the action can be initiated by the trainer who should be involved in any assessment.

When the action plan is produced at the end of the training event, the trainer

(a) contracts with the learner that a follow-up will take place after a period of some three or four months
(b) obtains the agreement of the learner that he will, on return to work, discuss the action plan with his boss and possibly provide him with a copy of the action plan
(c) obtains the agreement of the learner that the boss can also be contacted at the time of the follow-up.

Sometimes this contracting is unnecessary as, depending on the relationship developed between the trainer and the learner, the learner may request some or all of these steps without any prompting.

At the due time, a questionnaire based on the action plan is sent to the learner asking not only whether the action plan items have been implemented, but, if they have to give specific examples of the implementations. Also the learner is asked, if some of the action plan items have not been implemented or were not successful, why they were not implemented or how they were unsuccessful. A similar questionnaire is sent for the boss for comments as an external observer. It is again a matter of contracting whether both replies are seen by all the participating parties or whether some are made in confidence. As suggested earlier, peers or subordinates can also be brought in at this time, with the agreement of the learner, by sending them a questionnaire similar to that sent to the boss.

The use of follow-up questionnaires in the way described is an *indirect* form of follow-up; a more *direct* form is for the trainer to visit the learner and the boss to conduct in-depth interviews related to the implementation of the action plan.

There can be little doubt that the direct approach produces results far superior to the indirect questionnaire. In a direct confrontation, the trainer can probe for the exact details of any reported incidents and if relevant, elicit emotional as well as factual information. At an interview of this nature a follow-up action plan can often be formulated which commits the learner to action on items either not implemented or additional. There is the advantage that the boss can be directly involved at the construction of the second action plan.

However, the direct approach is not without disadvantages. It is, of course, essential that the trainer, or whoever conducts the follow-up, is a skilled depth interviewer who is able to probe below the immediate, superficial answers. But the principal disadvantage must relate to the involvement of resources, in terms of both people and time. If the course contained twelve members, this means a minimum of twelve visits. The learners may be scattered around the country, requiring the interviewer to travel long distances. Consequently it must be assumed that each interview will take at least a day and a half. To visit twelve people will involve a total minimum expenditure of time of eighteen days – far more than the length of the five day course! The arguments given must be cogent to justify this expenditure.

There are advantages to a direct approach as far as evaluation is concerned. If it is found, for example, that the action plan containing all the major items of training has been implemented in every way, this helps to confirm firstly the learning and secondly the validity of the training. But remember always the possible contaminations.

A last factor which must be considered in relation to action plans is the possible 'action gap' between the euphoria at the end of the course when the action plan was produced and what happens when the learner returns to the real world of work. The attitudes of boss, peers and subordinates in this real world can range from apathy, through passive neutrality to active alienation and rejection of the learner's newly-acquired skills, ideas and beliefs. The learner's relationship with the boss is particularly important which is why a prompt, post-course debriefing session between the boss and the learner is essential. During the meeting the learning can be discussed as well as the learner's intentions about the learning, that is the action plan. If, however, the boss will not support the learner, the learner may have problems progressing the action plan and maintaining motivation and interest.

Indirect observation questionnaires. The more usual evaluative approach at the intermediate stage, particularly when the learners are scattered throughout the country, is to use some form of questionnaire. The format will often depend on which one has been used previously with the learner. These could be questionnaires based on types such as the semantic differential, Thurstone, Likert, choice and so on. If the same format has been used consistently since the start of the course, during the course, at the end of the course and at the intermediate evaluation stage, although the answers may be subjective, at least they have been produced from the same base throughout and offer some degree of direct comparison.

One of these questionnaires and its use in human relations training was described in Chapter 8 (Figure 8.1.). This questionnaire was used pre-course and at the end of the course in the 3-Test approach. If the same questionnaire is used again at the follow-up stage, direct comparisons can be made with previous scoring indications.

Direct observation. Despite the comments made earlier concerning the expensive use of time and people, direct observation of activity must be the most effective method of evaluation. But the observer must know exactly what is being sought and must be skilled in the method of observation, otherwise unwanted subjective views can intrude.

Probably the most useful aid in this subsequent direct observation is the job or task analysis approach performed prior to the training event and described earlier. This is particularly so where the activities are severely practical rather than being more obtuse relationships. The example of practical observation described earlier was the hotel receptionist, an activity in which a considerable amount of the work is practical and observable.

At the follow-up stage the receptionist can be observed actually performing his duties. During this observation it can be recorded whether he is accomplishing his tasks in the way in which he was trained and whether he is doing this correctly. In this way, both the training and the effective execution of the task can be assessed.

Observation of the trained hotel receptionist against the job and task analysis is both difficult and complicated, and involves the use of some form of activity analysis or behaviour analysis. These analyses can then be compared with activity and behaviour patterns which have been assessed as effective. The more extensive and complicated the job, the greater the likelihood of contamination by factors not attributable to the training and the consequent increased difficulty of evaluating the true effect of the training.

Direct observation or activity sampling presents other problems. If a training task is long or complicated, the observer must remain with the worker long enough to observe at least one full cycle of the task. This will be particularly difficult if the job does not have a regular sequence of activities. The continuous presence of the observer may adversely affect the actions of the person being observed, particularly if the observer has to ask questions to determine *why* something is being done rather than just observing *what* is being done.

One method of reducing the long period of observation is the SISCO method used in a London School of Economics survey. SISCO stands for Standard Interval Sampling with

Continuous Observation. In this method the observer was recording every two minutes during a period of two hours, the periods being spread over the working day and the week. Obviously not every observational requirement will be met by this approach.

Depth interviews. Whatever the form of observation used it can be linked with a depth interview, or the depth interview approach can be used on its own, depending on circumstances. The interview has been referred to earlier when linked to the follow-up of action planning, but for evaluation purposes the interview can stand alone as the follow-up technique.

The approach to an interview at this stage is very similar to interviews held for many other reasons: particular emphasis is placed on probing questions designed to produce answers which are not superficial. A typical reply to an enquiry about progress can be 'Oh, I'm coming along very nicely'. This is too general an answer to be acceptable for evaluation, so an initial probing question could then be 'In what way do you feel you are coming along?'. The interview has two main aims: to identify what learning has taken place, and thus how effective the training has been, and how much of the learning has been put into effective practice.

Repertory Grid. The repertory grid can be considered as a particular form of depth interview in which, for the second or third time the interviewee produces his constructs from the same set of elements used on the previous occasions. The constructs of each grid can then be compared and analysed and from this comparison it may be able to detect any further changes of attitude. As an alternative, so that direct comparison can be made even easier, the grid can be used with the same elements and constructs, but on this occasion the interviewee is asked to reconsider his scoring scales.

Self-diaries. One method of deciding an individual's training needs is the completion of a diary before the training event. For a specific period the potential learner keeps an activity diary which details everything the learner does and how long is spent on each event. From an analysis of the diary entries it can be determined whether the learner is operating efficiently: is too much time being spent on tasks which could be delegated; are interruptions allowed; are meetings not planned sufficiently or are they planned too much; and so on.

At the follow-up stage the learner is required to repeat the diary completion for a comparable period. The second diary is then analysed to see if it reveals a more appropriate pattern of behaviour or skills.

The disadvantage of the diary method is that it depends on the honesty and integrity of the individual completing the diary. It is so easy to enter in the diary the items which *should* be entered rather than those which actually occur so that the completer is presented in the best possible light. This of course negates completely the value of the diary from the point of view of both the trainer and the learner. It does, however, reveal that the learner knows what should be entered in an effective diary; entries of this nature just *may* encourage him to actually behave in this way!

BUSINESS ASSESSMENT EVALUATION

Perhaps the most realistic method of evaluating the results of training is to try to assess effects in the business, if this is possible. If the training has been concerned with increasing the marketing skills of salesmen, the new level of sales can be assessed against the original level. If this level has increased, there is a suggestion that the training has been responsible for at least some of this improvement. It can only be a 'suggestion' that this improvement is due to the training as there may have been other 'non-attributable' factors at work.

Comparison with any changes in performance of a control group will help to make the evaluation more realistic, but as we have seen contamination can also occur with control comparisons of this nature. For example, should the control group of salesmen be concerned with the same product industry, it is possible that during the comparison period the product in the control group's firm or division may have improved and thus become more sellable. Or, unbeknownst to the trainer/evaluator, the control group or its leader may have decided that as it was a control group, it would make an all-out effort to beat the training group.

VALUE FOR MONEY

Assessment of the value for money given by the training has similar problems to the assessment of the amount of increased business described in the previous section. A simple cost evaluation consists of costs and benefits.

The costs are related to the charges made for the training. The costs involved in a learner attending a training course external to the employing organisation could include

- the fees charged to the organisation by the trainer
- the cost of travelling and accommodation involved
- costs incurred, notionally and actually, by the organisation's staff in connection with arrangements for the trainee's attendance
- the trainee's time
- loss of production as a result of the trainee's absence.

The costs of other forms of training are much more difficult to assess, particularly where some form of on-the-job project work or coaching is involved. In these cases, where real work is involved, it is difficult to separate the work content from an oncost of training content. Even more difficult to cost is the provision of in-house training, by company trainers for company trainees in company time on company premises. However, since exact costs are difficult to obtain, a reasonable estimate may be made.

The benefits to the organisation, on the other hand, are as difficult to assess in monetary terms as they are in product benefits.

Let us consider the example of a meter reader who has been trained to perform his duties. Before his training he needed to be accompanied by another reader to help him in his duties: this entailed two wages, one of which would be saved following the training – an obvious direct cost-benefit. Similarly, if before the training the meter reader required 6 hours to read 36 meters and after the training he was able to read 72 meters in that time, a further cost-benefit is obvious.

The meter reader case is a relatively straightforward one: most are much more complex and difficult, if not impossible to assess in terms of cost-benefits. Physical work activities by an individual can produce identifiable benefits but, even in the case of physical activities, complications arise when the learner is part of a working group. The evaluation becomes even more difficult, and often completely impossible, if the training has been of a human relations nature, or involving mental or social skills, or a mixture of these and physical activities.

Assessment at this post-training stage is principally concerned with evaluation (the total benefits) rather than simply validation of the training. Obviously there are many difficulties in the way of achieving this fully and in the long run it may be necessary to accept a subjective view, however much resource may have been poured into the assessment. The trainer or training manager must decide to what extent he must provide resources for this purpose, often very extensive and costly resources, in the full understanding of the degree of objectivity or quantitativeness which will be achieved.

LONG-TERM EVALUATION

If, as has been suggested earlier in this chapter, evaluation after the relatively short period of three to four months is very difficult if not impossible, then this view must be consolidated when evaluation is considered after an even longer interval. Warr, Bird and Rackham have in fact stated that at such levels the evaluation of training is usually impossible. However, others have suggested that it might be possible provided that the whole process has been subject to strict controls from the earliest stages. An approach is possible if a full task analysis has been obtained, specific training needs identified and tight training objectives set, end-of-course validation obtained and subsequent evaluation undertaken, with control activities at all stages.

In theory it makes little difference whether subsequent evaluation occurs after twelve months or longer, but obviously the longer the interval, the greater the likelihood of contamination through non-attributable factors.

Techniques. All the techniques employed at the mid-term evaluation can be repeated at this stage and there is considerable value in consistency. Perhaps the ideal is to use the same evaluation instrument throughout the complete process from pre-course, through post-course and mid-term to long-term. This enables a relatively simple and direct comparison of results and an approach can be made to some degree of objective measurement of change. It may not always be possible, of course, to be as consistent as this.

By the long-term stage, the emphasis has moved almost completely away from the validation of the training *per se* and is concentrating on the effect of the training on the effectiveness of the individual and hence the organisation. In the same way that the individual might be observed at the mid-term stage, so this process can be repeated at the long-term stage to show whether the skills have been maintained or improved, or whether they have regressed. We must not take too purist an attitude about these observations, particularly in view of the increased likelihood of contamination by non-attributable factors. If the skills have been maintained since the training, this shows that the training is still of value in the current performance of the job. If, on the other hand, they have improved, does it really matter why? In this instance the organisation is receiving a bonus since the individual is required only to *maintain* the trained level. At the other end of the scale, if the performance level has dropped since the mid-term evaluation, this can suggest that either the training has no long-term effects, or something has happened to the individual in the job to reduce his motivation to perform to the level to which he has been trained.

If the performance level has fallen, the emphasis of the evaluation must be to discover the answer to this problem. However, in terms of realistic evaluation the question 'Has the training benefited the organisation in economic or output terms?' must be answered. Most authorities on evaluation feel that in most instances, certainly above the simple practical level, it is impossible to answer this question. This will certainly be so in most cases of management training and many cases of social skills training.

This disappointing answer will be the only one possible at the completely objective level. But there is good reason to accept a subjective assessment, provided we remember that it is subjective: it may be the only one we are able to obtain! The individual's line manager is in a unique position to make the day-to-day assessment, and in many organisations is forced to do so by the annual appraisal system. At the very least, if at an appraisal subsequent to the training the individual's level of performance has not gone down, but has improved, some of this improvement may be due to the training. Skilled questioning may help to elicit, albeit subjectively, the degree of this effect.

What is the alternative to the approaches discussed in this book? It is surely to conclude that validation and evaluation are too expensive in time, resources and money, and will not necessarily produce an objective assessment – so they are not attempted, and no objective measures at all are available to help the training which occurs at considerable cost. This decision can be taken by the organisation in the same way that it could decide to contribute to *any* form of training. Obviously some attempt at assessment must be made.

Who does the evaluation? There is little controversy over who performs the training and who manages an individual, but it is certainly far from clear who should be involved in the different stages of the validation and evaluation. A complete system is costly in terms of staff time and resources.

If only the trainer is involved, more time may have to be spent on evaluation than training; if only the manager is involved there will be little time for him to manage. An external assessor can be introduced who can follow the system with complete neutrality and bringing expertise to the evaluation, but such individuals are rare and can be unacceptably costly if they have to get to know the organisation as well as follow an evaluation approach from start to finish. It will be less costly if such an expert is already employed within the organisation, say a psychologist, but even then there is a substantial notional and actual cost.

The most realistic approach will be to have an amalgamation of at least the trainer and the line manager, with, preferably, some support from the neutral assessor. There are many permutations of this combination and one realistic approach could be:

> Pre-course. Analysis and identification of needs: trainer and manager.
> During course and at end of course. Trainer.
> Control group. Throughout: external assessor.
> Mid-term. Trainer to some extent, but more particularly the line manager.
> Long-term. External assessor and line manager.

Whatever permutation might be used and how much subjectivity might be acceptable, the important aspects of validation and evaluation are that

(a) Some form of validation and evaluation should be attempted
(b) There must be as much co-operation between the trainer and line manager as possible, for, after all, the manager is the first line client and the trainer the provider.

APPENDIX ONE
THE EVALUATION
PROCESS

Suspect existence of a problem

↓

Consider job description to identify job needs

↓

Produce job specification

↓

Conduct job and task analysis

↓

Identify errors and omissions

=

Training needs

↓

Determine most effective method of learning

↓

Test existing skills, knowledge, attitudes

↓

Conduct training event

↓

Immediate reaction testing

↓

Session, section, day reviews
↓
End of course testing of skills, knowledge, attitudes
↓
End of course validation review
↓
Mid-term evaluation follow-up

+ boss,
peers,
subordinates

↓
Long-term evaluation follow-up
↓
Identify control group(s)
↓
Test existing skills etc.
↓
Second testing of skills etc.
↓
Third testing of skills etc.
↓
Fourth testing of skills etc.

APPENDIX TWO
PRACTICAL
APPLICATIONS

Techniques and methods of validation and evaluation have been applied to training and development in this book. However, it takes very little modification to transfer the application to other activities.

A practical example of this can be the personal evaluation of this book by the reader! Obviously we can do nothing about the identification of needs; these must be assumed by the fact that you have read the book. Nor can we do anything *now* about mid-term and long-term evaluation; the reader should be able to do this for himself. However, we can do something positive in terms of the immediate outcome level, both as internal and external validation.

As an example, limited use can be made of a control group. Take one aspect from the book which was new to you and about which you have learned. Then ask some people who have not read the book – people who can be directly compared with you in a range of aspects, such as age, training, experience, and so on – what they know about the aspect selected. This is your control group.

Another possible approach is to assess one's immediate personal reaction to the book (training). This can be attempted by completing the type of questionnaire discussed in the book. Reproduced here is a limited questionnaire of this nature. It is purely for your own self-assessment and interest, but if you care to send a copy to me via the publisher, I would be very interested to receive it.

Place a ✓ in what you feel is the most appropriate space for each scale. For example └──┴─✓┴──┴──┴──┘

1. I found the reading of this book

Easy └──┴──┴──┴──┴──┘ Difficult

2. I found understanding the material in the book

Easy └──┴──┴──┴──┴──┘ Difficult

3. Before reading the book my knowledge of the subject was

A lot └──┴──┴──┴──┴──┘ Nothing

4. Having read the book I now rate my knowledge of the subject as

A lot └──┴──┴──┴──┴──┘ Nothing

5. The range of material in the book was

Too wide └──┴──┴──┴──┴──┘ Too narrow

6. What interested me in the book overall was

Everything └──┴──┴──┴──┴──┘ Nothing

7. The presentation of the material in the book was

Very interesting └──┴──┴──┴──┴──┘ Boring

8. The presentation of the material in the book was

Too
academic └──────┴──────┴──────┴──────┴──────┘ Too
practical

9. The book satisfied the objectives of the author, as set out below.

Fully └──────┴──────┴──────┴──────┴──────┘ Not at all

10. My overall assessment of the book is

Very
good └──────┴──────┴──────┴──────┴──────┘ Very
poor

Please add any other assessments you wish to make. Thank you.

OBJECTIVES (REFER TO APPENDIX 2)

1. To survey the range of validation and evaluation approaches available to the training assessor from the identification of training needs to long-term evaluation.

2. To demonstrate the range of validation and evaluation instruments available.

3. To provide a practical guide for practising training assessors.

4. To introduce some validation and evaluation methods not in common use but which can be used with value.

REFERENCES AND RECOMMENDED READING

Annett, Duncan, Stammers and Gray, *Task Analysis*, Training Information Paper 6, HMSO, 1971.

Boydell, T. H., *A Guide to the Identification of Training Needs*, BACIE, 1976.

This booklet considers the important aspect that the identification of training needs must be resolved before training can be undertaken. Models for the consideration of present and future training needs are presented in a practical way and a variety of processes and approaches are described.

Boydell, T. H., *A Guide to Job Analysis*, BACIE, 1970.

A companion booklet to The Identification of Training Needs. It describes a process for job analysis which, although specifically applicable to operative, craft, clerical and technician occupations, when used in conjunction with other approaches in management development, is relevant also to supervisory and management activities.

Davies, I. K., *The Management of Learning*, McGraw-Hill, 1971. (Chapters 14 and 15.)

Chapter 14 of this book is concerned with the evaluation of a learning course and discusses criterion tests and tests of educational achievement, and looks at the nature, importance and techniques of evaluation. Chapter 15 looks at the measurement of learning in terms of nominal, ordinal, intervals and ratio scales and criterion power tests. Formulae are given for the various test types and the different types of scoring are compared.

Easterby-Smith, M., Braiden, E. M., *and* Ashton D., *Auditing Management Development*, Gower, 1980.

The 'audit' approach to the effectiveness of training and development is described with the use and analysis of special questionnaires or audit instruments. Descriptions of actual audits undertaken are also given.

Easterby-Smith, M., 'How to Use Repertory Grids in HRD' *Journal of European Industrial Training*, Vol 4, No 2, 1980.

Hamblin, A. C., *The Evaluation and Control of Training*, McGraw-Hill, 1974.

One of the few published books specifically devoted to evaluation, it is intended to be a link between how-to-do-it approaches and theoretical dissertations. Hamblin aims the book at training specialists and bases his discussions on a cycle of evaluation of objectives and effects. A range of techniques at each level is discussed.

Honey, P., 'The Repertory Grid in Action', *Industrial and Commercial Training*, Vol II, Nos 9, 10 and 11, 1979.

Kelly, G. A., *The Psychology of Personal Constructs*, Norton, 1953.

The original work by Kelly in which he introduces the concepts of personal constructs and domains from which the repertory grid techniques were developed.

Kirkpatrick, D. L., 'Evaluation of Training' in *Training and Development Handbook*, edited by R. L. Craig, McGraw-Hill, 1976.

Laird, D., *Approaches to Training and Development*, Addison-Wesley, 1978. (Chapters 15 and 16.)

A book which covers the spectrum of training and development approaches and contains two chapters on (Chapter 15) instruments for measuring training and development and (Chapter 16) a discussion on the wider aspects of evaluation.

Mager, R. F., *Preparing Objectives for Programmed Instruction*, Fearon, 1962. (Later re-titled: *Preparing Instructional Objectives*, Fearon, 1975).

Manpower Services Commission, 'A Glossary of Training Terms', HMSO, 1981.

Odiorne, G. S., *Training by Objectives*, Macmillan, 1970.

The specific setting of objectives and the need to achieve these objectives are discussed as the positive indicators of training effectiveness and success.

Parker, T. C., 'Statistical Methods for Measuring Training Results' in *Training and Development Handbook*, edited by R. L. Craig, McGraw-Hill, 1976.

Rackham, N. and Morgan, T., *Behaviour Analysis in Training*, McGraw-Hill, 1977.

This book, by two of the initiators of Behaviour Analysis, describes the BA approach to interactive skills training and discusses the use of BA in the testing, immediate reaction and validation approaches to this training. A chapter (Chapter 5) is devoted to the subject of evaluation and many examples of interactive skills training evaluation in practice are cited.

Rackham, N. and others, *Developing Interactive Skills*, Wellens, 1971.

This book was in many ways the predecessor to *Behaviour Analysis in Training* as it introduced the concept of BA and its use in training. Some mention is made of the use of BA in evaluation.

Rae, L. *The Skills of Training*, Gower, 1983. (Chapter 10.)

This book, which is an introduction to training approaches, methods and techniques summarises in Chapter 10 the trainer's approach to validation and evaluation, and introduces some of the approaches.

Rae, L., 'Towards a More Valid End-of-Course Validation', *The Training Officer*, October 1983.

Rae, L., 'The Validation of Training', *Training and Development*, May 1984.

Rae, L., *The Skills of Human Relations Training*, Gower, 1985.

A companion book to *The Skills of Training*, it contains a chapter describing the possible evaluation and validation approaches possible to subjective subjects such as those contained in the book.

Rae, L., 'How Valid is Validation?,' *Industrial and Commercial Training*, Jan.–Feb., 1985.

Robinson, K. R., *A Handbook of Training Management*, Kogan Page, 1981. (Chapter 7).

A substantial chapter (Chapter 7) is included in the book on the measurement and follow-up of the results of training process. It also considers the 'biggest headache a training manager has', namely the measurement and assessment of the training for which the manager is responsible.

Smith, M. and Ashton, D., 'Using Repertory Grid Techniques to Evaluate Management Training', *Personnel Review*, Vol 4, No 4, 1975.

Stewart, V. and Stewart, A., *Managing the Manager's Growth*, Gower, 1978. (Chapter 13).

Another book of the general management training and development nature which includes a chapter (Chapter 13) on evaluation, presented in the very readable style of the Stewarts. A broad approach is taken although a number of specific methods are also discussed.

Thurley, K. E. and Wirdenius, H., *Supervision: a Reappraisal*, Heinemann, 1973.

Warr, P. B., Bird, M. and Rackham, N., *The Evaluation of Management Training*, Gower, 1970.

One of the few books devoted to the subject. It offers a strongly practical approach to validation and evaluation, identifying the needs in a framework called CIRO which emphasises context, input, reaction and outcome evaluation, the latter having three levels of immediate, intermediate and ultimate outcomes.

Whitelaw, M., *The Evaluation of Management Training: a Review*, Institute of Personnel Management, 1972.

The third book contained in this list devoted completely to evaluation. The contents are only marginally of an original nature as the publication sets out to be a review of the subject. Some methods of evaluation are described, principally at the three outcome levels and some useful summaries of some classical studies are given. A very extensive bibliography over the period 1939 to 1971 is included, listing publications ranging from Personnel Psychology, Journal of Applied Psychology and Journal of Abnormal and Social Psychology, through Journal of the Academy of Management and the Harvard Business Review, to the Industrial and Commercial Training Journal and the Journal of the Institute of Training and Development.

INDEX

Accommodation 9
Action centred learning 89
Action planning 110, 128
    contracting 128
Activity analysis 89
Activity observation 87, 89
Activity sampling 131
Agreement to observational
    analysis 30
Aims 23
Amount of learning 9
Analysis of training needs 18, 26
    knowledge 26, 35
    skills 28, 34
    social attitudes 28
    social skills 28
Analysis interviews 31
Application of learning 10
Appraisal interview observation
    59, 64, 66
Appraisal interview effective
    behaviour 66
Attitude self-assessment 82
Audio aids 92
Audits 17, 36, 97

Behaviour analysis 59, 69, 94, 116
Behaviour categories 59
Behaviour data feedback 95

Behaviour definitions 61
Behaviour observation 57
Behaviour observation forms 64
Behaviour skills questionnaire 82
Benefits of training 134
Binary choice 75, 114
Bird, M. 3, 4, 135
Blank sheet review 107
Brainstorming 39
Business assessment 133

Category lists 60
Client interest 8
Co-counselling 33
Content of training 9
Control groups 71, 127
Costs of training 134
Course daily audits 97
Critical incident technique 39
Critical person approach 39

Daily audits 97
Data feedback 95
De Bono, E. 39
Definitions
    assessment of training
        effectiveness 3
    evaluation 3, 4, 5
    validation 3, 5

Delayed validation 112, 126
Delphi technique 36
Depth interviews 132
Diaries 38, 132
Direct observation evaluation 130

Effective behaviour patterns 66
Efficiency 10
End of course questionnaires 99,
　　105, 108
Examination question approach
　　74, 114
External validation 113

Feelings review 108
Feasibility 1
Fishbowl observation 88

Group observation 87
Group review 104

Hamblin, A.C. 4
Happiness sheets 107, 125
Hindsight 10

Identification of training needs
　　12, 14, 16
　　who identifies them? 13
Immediate outcome evaluation 4
Immediate reaction 4
Immediate validation 112
Inclusion of others 112, 126
Indirect observation 130
Initial assessments 72, 79, 83
Input evaluation 3
Interaction analysis 66
Intermediate outcome 4
Internal validation 3, 104
Interviews 31, 53, 89, 112, 132
　　observation 89

Job analysis 18, 41
Job data collection 21, 26
Job descriptions 18, 29
Job specifications 20, 22, 26, 29

Kelly, G.A. 42
Knowledge analysis 26
　　questionnaire 27
Knowledge increase assessment
　　113
Knowledge initial assessment 73
Knowledge tests 27, 74, 113

Learning transfer 9
Length of training 9
Likert scale 99, 116, 130
Long-term evaluation 135

Mager, R.F. 24
Management development 36
Management Training Index 8
Method of training 9
Mirroring 40
Morgan, T. 66
Multiple choice tests 76, 114

Non-verbal behaviour 30

Objectives 9, 24
Observational analysis 28, 30
Observation support 31
Obtaining agreement 30
Omissions 9
One-to-one interaction observa-
　　tion 89
Open answer tests 74, 114
Open assessments 107
Output evaluation 3
Over-use of tests 101

Performance 29
Performance questionnaire 39
Practical application 114
Pre-course testing 74
Pre/Post test 117, 118
Profile feedback 95
Process observation 56
Psychological tests 41

Questions to ask 8
Questionnaires 27, 34, 37, 79, 83

Rackham, N. 3, 4, 66, 135
Repertory Grid 42, 116, 132
　　constructs 43
　　elements 43
　　in practice 44
　　interviewer intervention 53
　　problems 54
　　scoring 44, 48
　　steps 44

Self-assessment 79, 82
Semantic differential question-
　　naire 79, 99, 106, 116, 130
Semi-structured interview 32

Senior manager interest 7
Session assessment 98
Short-answer tests 78, 114
SISCO 131
Skills analysis 28, 34
  listing 34
  questionnaire 34
Skill assessment 73, 78, 114
Staged questionnaire 99
Structured interview 32

Task analysis 18
Three-test approach 118
Three-words audit 97
Thurstone scale 81, 99, 117, 130
Trainee-centred training 14
Trainer-centred training 14
Trainer interest 5

Trainer role 14, 15
Trainer skills 9
Training manager interest 6
Training needs 11, 13
Training objectives 22
Training specifications 22
True/false tests 76
Tutor assessments 100

Ultimate outcome evaluation 4
Unstructured interviews 32

Value for money 134
Verbal behaviour 30
Video equipment 92

Warr, P.B. 3, 4, 135
Who does the evaluation? 137